THE PAN

THE PAN BOOK OF CATS

ROSE TENENT

Revised edition

Pan Books London and Sydney

First published 1958 by Pan Books Ltd
Cavaye Place, London SW10 9PG
2nd printing (Revised) 1963
3rd printing (Revised) 1976

ISBN 0 330 24236 9
Printed and bound in Great Britain by
Richard Clay (The Chaucer Press) Ltd, Bungay, Suffolk

CONTENTS

ACKNOWLEDGEMENTS

I should like to express my gratitude to all who have supplied illustrations for this book. My thanks are also due to Mrs Alison Ashford for her help with the chapter on Rex cats, and to the Governing Council of the Cat Fancy for allowing me to quote and draw upon their Standards of Points for the respective breeds.

LIST OF ILLUSTRATIONS

(between pages 64 and 65)

CHINCHILLA
Name: Jingles of Thame. Bred by Mrs McLeod.
Owner: Mrs Loughborough. *Photo: Mrs V. E. Major*

CREAM PERSIAN AND KITTENS
Name: Hathaway Antony Roly, with some of his kittens.
Owner: Mrs Rowena Ross. *Photo: Keith Marshall*

SILVER TABBY LONG-HAIR
Name: Ch. Purring Gentle Faith.
Owned and bred by Miss E. L. Jury.
Photo: Welbeck Photography

ABYSSINIANS
Name: Ch. Kreeoro Sheba (and son).
Photo: Mrs V. E. Major

DOG AND CAT FRIENDSHIP
Mrs Sheila Ball's Francesca Lisblanc (Pyrenean Mountain Dog), Champion Carreg Clover (White Persian) and Lisblanc Dwani and Lisblanc Donna (Siamese Cats).
Photo: Lancelot Vining

WHITE SHORT-HAIR
Name: Whitehaugh Cream Cracker.
Owner: Miss Ann L. Stubbs. *Photo: Tony Hunt*

WHITE PERSIAN
Name: Dalmond Impudence. Bred by Mrs M. E. Dallison.
Owner: the late King Feisal of Iraq. *Photo: R. Collins*

WHITE MANX
Name: Scylla.
Owner: Mrs F. M. Twining, St Johns, IOM

PERSIAN KITTENS
Photo: Studio Lisa, Ltd

BLACK PERSIAN
Name: Bourneside Black Cloris. Bred by Mrs E. G. Aitken.
Photo: Ludgate Garden Photographers

BLUE PERSIAN
Name: Ch. Bayhorne Ajax.
Owned and bred by Mrs Dulcie Benbow.

SEAL-POINTED SIAMESE
Name: Ch. Killdown Sultan.
Owner: Miss Daphne J. Wells. *Photo: Walton Adams*

CHAPTER 1

ACQUIRING A CAT

WHAT IS more homely than a well-fed, glossy-coated cat stretched out on the hearthrug? Dainty and dignified, the cat makes an ideal companion, for even if it accepts no favours it is very grateful for affection. As Théophile Gautier said: 'A cat will be your friend, but never your slave'.

The prospect of acquiring a cat is always exciting. Those of us who are animal lovers always know of someone who is looking for a good home for a cat or kitten. Therefore the easiest way is to accept the gift of a friend. Whether your new pet is a handsome aristocrat, such as a Siamese or Blue Persian, or just an 'ordinary' bonny kitten does not matter in the least. Given a welcome and understanding it will show you the same loyalty and devotion.

So will the cat you adopt from an animal welfare society or the starved-looking stray which appears at your back door. Such cats naturally may be anything but attractive on first appearance, although many of them grow into beautiful animals when given proper care. Not only do they become exceptionally gentle and affectionate towards their owners, but they are usually very self-reliant and clean. They also make excellent mousers.

Make sure of course that the cat you befriend really is a stray, because some cats will visit regularly anyone who is kind-hearted enough to feed them. The genuine stray is almost always a pitiful sight. It may creep timidly towards the house in search of any scraps it hopes your own pampered pets will have left uneaten. But if you are about it will rarely venture inside. In fact it will probably dash off at the sight of any human. Several days, or even weeks, may pass before you are allowed to stroke it; perhaps longer before it purrs for you.

The animal welfare shelters nearly always have cats queueing up for good homes. Here is but one selection from the 'Homes Wanted' column of *The Cat*, official journal of the Cats' Protection League, fuller particulars of which are given in Chapter 8.

Kind owners wanted for:

1. A gentle, friendly little cat.
2. A very shy cat.
3. A big, bold, handsome hunter.
4. A very plain cat, but haughty as a beauty.
5. A very pretty cat.
6. A bomb-site stray, friendly and cheerful.
7. A handsome creature whose owner is going abroad.
8. A very pretty cat whose owner cannot keep her in new home.
9. A cheeky little fellow rescued from a fierce dog.
10. A real pet, found wandering, but never claimed.

A note was added that each of the above cats was young, healthy, neutered and fully-house-trained. What better way of acquiring a cat?

However, perhaps you want a more unusual cat. You may have seen a particularly fluffy kitten in a pet-shop window. Or possibly you favour a pedigree cat with a view to breeding or exhibiting.

If you know the breed you want, it is a good idea to write to the Secretary of the Governing Council of the Cat Fancy (the organisation which looks after the interests of cats much as the Kennel Club does for dogs), Mrs W. Davis, Dovefields, Petworth Road, Witley, Surrey, and ask to be put in touch with the secretary of the respective breed club. Naturally you will enclose a stamped, self-addressed envelope for this service. You can then apply to the club secretary for names of breeders in, or near, your neighbourhood who may have kittens for sale.

An alternative method is to follow the advertisements in the appropriate columns of the Press. Notices of cats for sale appear from time to time in national and local newspapers, weekly journals such as *The Lady*, *The Queen*, *Exchange and Mart*, *Country Life*, and the quarterly magazine, *The Countryman*. Similar adverts will be found in *Fur and Feather* (official organ of the Cat Fancy), published fortnightly from Idle, Bradford.

At the time of writing there are more than 60 breeds from which to choose. These are divided into two groups, Long-haired cats (commonly known as Persians) and Short-haired cats, which can be either British or foreign type. You will find a description of all the breeds in Chapters 9–12.

If you are undecided between several breeds, or perhaps are not quite sure of the difference, then your best plan (after reading Chapters 9–12) is to visit a cat show. At an all-breed show you will be able to see the different varieties in their pens and to learn something of their characteristics from the breeders. Do not be shy of asking these people questions. You will find that they are only too happy to help.

Cat shows are held all over Britain and are advertised in *Fur and Feather*, the address of which has been given. The shows are held mostly during the autumn and winter. This is because the cats are then in full coat, and also because the brood queens (in the Cat Fancy female cats are known as queens) are not so busy rearing their families as they would be in the spring and summer.

However, there are one or two exceptions. Chief of these is the Kensington Kitten and Neuter Cat Club's Show, held annually in London, usually in July. If, as I did, you can make this your first show, you will certainly enjoy it. The title of this show explains its purpose. There you will find the finest examples of every breed.

Of course you need not necessarily buy your kitten at the show. But if you decide to do so, then you will not be able to take it home until the allotted time. Personally, I think it is a good idea to choose a kitten at a show and to arrange with the breeder that you collect it from his (or her) address a few days later. In this way it has time to settle down in its original surroundings after the excitement of the show atmosphere.

What you pay for your cat or kitten will depend on the breed. Also, whether you want just a pet kitten or a show cat. Therefore, be sure to tell the breeder exactly what you require. A reputable breeder will not risk his (or her) reputation by trying to sell you a prospective show cat if he has not one available, whatever price you are prepared to pay. On the other hand, he may be able to offer a choice of several kittens of the 'companion' variety, and at a very reasonable fee, provided you can guarantee a good home.

There will be nothing wrong with any of these kittens. The difference is that they will not excel in what are known as show points.

Most breeders, you will find, offer kittens for sale. Only very rarely will they part with an adult cat. When they do, there is often a waiting list of would-be purchasers all willing to pay a good price. This is understandable, especially if the cat is a well-known prize-winner. Nevertheless, there are occasions when a breeder is compelled, for personal reasons, to reduce his (or her) stock. In such cases a good home for the animal is almost always the first consideration.

Normally a kitten is the better proposition. It is true that some adult cats are not a bit nervous about going to new owners and will settle down almost immediately. However, a much larger number take months to adapt themselves to new surroundings. Stories of cats walking miles to be near former owners are legion. One of my own cats – a lovely sleek-coated tabby – disappeared from its temporary home while I was on holiday. The people I left it with were great cat lovers and could not have been kinder. Fortunately the cat was found sitting on my doorstep!

A kitten, on the other hand, will give you its companionship from infancy. Of course, it may take up a little more of your time than the adult cat. It will also be more mischievous.

But who would miss the fun of rearing a tiny cat and watching it during the prettiest time of its life? All too soon it will grow up and forsake its string-games for more sedate pleasures.

Should you have a Long-haired or a Short-haired kitten? This is entirely a matter of taste. Always remember, however, that if a Persian cat is to keep its beautiful, long silky coat, it will need constant grooming. If your time is limited, then a Short-haired cat is definitely the wiser choice.

If you fancy a female cat, do not allow the possibility of her recurring families to deter you. Nowadays a female kitten is easily made neuter. The operation is known as spaying, and provided it is performed by a skilled veterinary surgeon it should leave no ill effects upon the cat.

The most suitable age for spaying is from about 4 to 5 months, but it can be done successfully at any later age, even after a litter of kittens. A general anaesthetic will be necessary and the vet may want to keep your pet overnight. More often, however, he will allow it to return home the same day, knowing that cats usually make quicker progress in familiar surroundings. No special attention except warmth is normally required. Follow the vet's instructions, and do not allow your pet to get over-excited. She will then be quite all right.

A spayed female is to be particularly recommended where there are children. Gentle and affectionate, she makes a delightful pet.

Do not allow anyone to persuade you that it is wrong to neuter a male kitten. Unless you want your cat for breeding purposes (see Chapter 5), this minor operation is most advisable. The undoctored tom cat strays away for days, perhaps weeks, and spends much of its time fighting. It looks miserable and uncared for. But even if you do not mind this, the full male, however well behaved in kittenhood, usually, sooner or later, develops the unfortunate habit of spraying. When this happens it is no longer pleasant to have your pet with you in the house.

Neutering is best done when a kitten is about 4 months old, though it can be done successfully at any age. The operation consists of removing the testicles, and if performed too early both testicles may not have come down. The result will then be a failure. A general anaesthetic is used, but it is a slighter operation than spaying a female, and the cat will be its normal self almost immediately. Neutering should never be entrusted to anyone but a veterinary surgeon.

It is a fallacy that neutered cats become fat or lazy. Provided they are properly fed this is not so. Please believe that your cat will be a better pet for neutering – more contented, affectionate and full of character.

When you buy a kitten you want a healthy one, so choose the strongest and most active in the litter. Make sure it is at least 2 months old and properly weaned. Ask to see the mother and, if possible, get some particulars of the father. You will be given the kitten's pedigree, but just at first this may not convey much more than a series of names.

If there is only one kitten for disposal make certain it is lively. The fur should be soft and silky, and there should be no signs of flea-dirt when it is parted. Eyes should be bright – watery eyes indicate low condition. Brownish discharge inside the ears means canker, and while this is curable it can be very obstinate meanwhile, causing the cat much suffering.

Look at the kitten's tummy – if swollen, this may mean rickets or worms. It is true that many kittens do have roundworms, but they hinder the kitten's growth, and may even cause fits. Suggestions will be given later on for keeping a cat free from worms, but it is better not to start with this trouble.

Finally, make sure that there are no signs of recent diarrhoea. Again this is curable, but much patience may be needed.

Before you take your kitten home ask the breeder if it has been injected against Feline Infectious Enteritis. This is the most dreaded of all cat illness, details of which are given in Chapter 3. There is no cause for alarm, for probably your pet will never succumb to it, but should there be an outbreak in your neighbourhood, young cats are the most susceptible. Personally, I feel it is a sensible precaution to have a kitten immunised. There are several vaccines available. Your vet will advise.

Unless you live within walking distance from the breeder you will need a basket to take your kitten home. It is *not* a good idea to carry a kitten in your arms through crowded thoroughfares, in buses or across busy railway stations. The noise and bustle can be very frightening for such a tiny cat and may even upset its nerves for life. Cat baskets can be obtained from pet shops and livestock departments of London and Provincial stores. I always buy mine from the Homeworkers Department of the Royal London Society for Teaching and Training the Blind – 105–9 Salusbury Road, London, N.W.6.

Line your basket with several layers of newspaper and cover with a piece of soft, clean blanket. Put the kitten gently inside and fasten the basket securely. If you line the four sides of the basket with thick brown paper this will help to keep out draughts. It will also act as an extra precaution against those frightening sights and sounds.

CHAPTER 2

CARE AND FEEDING

THE FIRST thing a kitten usually wants to do is to explore the house. So accompany it on this voyage of exploration, then offer it a drink of milk. By now it will be sleepy, so you can put it on its bed. Stroke it gently; it will begin to purr! It has accepted you!

An adult cat may need a little more encouragement. If it seems nervous, then keep it in a quiet room for a day or two. Visit it from time to time with food, stroke it and talk quietly to it. Gradually persuade it to follow you about the house, making sure first that the outside doors are closed. Give it all the privileges you can in the way of warmth, comfort and affection. You will find that it will soon respond and return your friendship.

Whether cat or kitten, it will need a bed, and this, of course, you will have in readiness. All that is necessary for a young kitten is a cardboard box, with a piece cut out of the side, so that he can get in and out easily. The box should be raised a few inches from the ground to secure your pet from draughts. For bedding use several sheets of newspaper, which in itself is very warm. But cover them with a piece of soft, clean blanket, just in case the kitten licks the newsprint.

A grown cat will need a larger box. Or, you can buy him a basket, preferably with a hood or canopy, so that he will feel secure. The basket should have a cushion with a washable cover, and be placed in some draught-free corner where it won't be in the way. Do not encourage your cat to get on the family beds. It's best to shut him out of bedrooms. Also, if you have a young baby in the house, put a net over the cot and pram.

Near the sleeping-box your cat should be able to find its sanitary tray. Cats are extremely clean, and a kitten's mother will have taught it house-manners. All you need to do is to put the tray down. Your pet will understand.

Should a kitten misbehave, do not slap it. This may not cure the trouble, but it *will* make the kitten nervous. Naturally you should rebuke it, showing it the place where it has offended. Then put it on its tray. The lapses will soon cease.

Zinc and plastic trays can be bought from pet shops, but a meat tin or enamel baking dish will do. Fill this with dry earth, sand, peat-moss litter or sifted ashes. If you live in a flat you will probably find that peat-moss litter, or one of the proprietary cat litters, is most suitable because it is so easily disposed of after use.

Some people favour sawdust for the sanitary tray. Personally, I would not recommend this, as it is inclined to stick to the cat's fur, and may be swallowed when the animal washes itself. Also, if your cat is a Long-haired variety, the sawdust could tangle the fur and spoil your pet's appearance.

Clean the pan with a non-poisonous household disinfectant such as Dettol, Sanitas or TCP. The pan should be cleaned regularly and the material inside it renewed daily. No self-respecting cat will use a dirty pan.

Where there is a garden, your cat will soon learn to use it. The sanitary pan will then be necessary only at night time or in bad weather. Sunshine is the very best tonic for cats and kittens, so never coddle a cat. Let it play outside as much as possible. In that way it will build up resistance to possible infection.

Should your cat wear a collar? I would not risk spoiling the appearance of a Long-haired cat by putting a collar on him. But a Short-haired cat looks very smart in one. But be sure that it is partly made of elastic, as recommended by the Animal Welfare Societies. Then, if your cat goes climbing, he can free himself should the collar get caught in a branch of a tree.

Such collars are usually about half an inch wide, and bear a disc for the owner's name, address and telephone number. It is not advisable to have your cat's name on the collar, because it might be used by some unscrupulous person to entice him away.

How are you going to feed your cat? Never imagine that a cat will be a better mouser if it is underfed. Cats hunt for sport, and hunting, like any other job of work, requires strength. In order to work well a cat needs nourishment. And please do not think that scraps or saucers of milk will do. Of course there is no reason why your cat should not have left-over pieces of meat or fish (provided they are still fresh) as *additional* items in its diet. Also, if your cat likes milk (not all do, by any means), it will welcome this as an occasional treat. Too much milk may cause digestive trouble or skin complaints.

As a guide to correct diet, think of the cat in its natural environment. It is a carnivorous (flesh-eating) animal, with cusped teeth, which means that these are particularly adapted for tearing up meat. When the wild cat is hungry it goes in search of its prey, when thirsty it drinks from streams. In short, the cat's natural diet is meat and water.

Nevertheless, in the domesticated state it is advisable to make certain additions to this basic diet, especially in towns, where a cat is unable to hunt extra food for itself. Your pet should not be allowed to get too thin, as it undoubtedly would if fed only on raw meat. On the other hand – and this is particularly important if you wish to show a cat – it certainly must never be allowed to become too fat. Your cat's daily diet should contain protein, fats, vitamins, minerals and some carbohydrates to keep it in good health.

Let us begin by suggesting a suitable diet for a two-months-old kitten. Because your kitten has such a small tummy it cannot digest much food at once. On the other hand, it digests its food very quickly. If too few meals are given it becomes very hungry and over-eats, the result being diarrhoea or vomiting. The answer then is frequent food but in very small quantities.

From 2 to 4 months old a kitten needs 4 to 5 tiny meals a day. These should be nourishing and well-balanced. The best way is to give milky food and solid food in alternation. Opinion varies considerably as to whether a kitten should be fed raw meat before it is 4 months old. Therefore, whenever possible, find out from the previous owner how your kitten has been fed. Most breeders will gladly provide a feeding-chart, and this is a good idea, because any sudden change of diet may upset a kitten's tummy. There is not the slightest reason why you should not make changes, but do this gradually. At first be guided by the breeder.

If advice is not obtainable, then be on the safe side and cook the meat. Mince it before feeding, or cut it up very fine. Fish and rabbit should always be cooked, then chopped or cut up into tiny pieces. When fish or rabbit are given it is essential to remove the bones. A large, non-splinter bone is good for a kitten's teeth, but fish and poultry bones are very dangerous. They can lodge in a kitten's throat and choke it, or splinter in its stomach and cause great suffering, even death.

Now for the menu. Suppose you feed milk at breakfast time, then you could give your pet a little boiled or steamed fish for lunch. If you add a few brown breadcrumbs these will provide roughage and also help to absorb any surplus moisture. At tea time your kitten might have a little brown bread and milk, cereal and milk, or cereal which has been moistened with warm water flavoured by something like Yeastrel, Marmite or Vecon. For supper you could give a little minced meat or cooked rabbit. With the exception of milky meals, the food should always be given on the dry side. Never feed milk and meat together, or you are asking for digestive troubles. And because not all kittens can digest cow's milk, it's advisable to thicken it with something like baby-food, cornflakes or egg-yolk. Never feed frozen food or lumpy food. Milk should be slightly warmed.

You will find that your kitten makes better progress if you add a drop or two of halibut-liver oil to each of the solid meals. This is particularly beneficial if you acquire your kitten in winter, when it will need extra vitamins to make up for any possible deficiency of sunshine. Halibut-liver oil is rich in vitamins A and D, which are so necessary towards healthy growth and good bone development. If you prefer, you can give the halibut-liver oil in capsule form – one capsule a day.

I would also give a kitten half a yeast tablet daily, broken over the food. As your pet grows, increase the ration until, at 5 or 6 months old, it is getting 2 or 3 tablets a day. Yeast contains vitamin B and valuable mineral salts. It will help the kitten to digest its food and greatly enhance its appearance. Veterinary yeast can be obtained from chemists and pet stores. You should have no difficulty in persuading your pet to take them. Most cats will eat them like sweets.

From about 4 months old gradually introduce other food into the menu. For example, a little cooked carrot or green vegetable could be added to the main meal. Mince this up with the meat so that it is not too obvious. Most kittens enjoy a little grated cheese. Almost all appreciate a sardine or lightly-boiled liver. Do not feed these too often, however, because they have a laxative effect.

As your pet grows out of kittenhood it will need fewer meals but larger quantities. At 5 or 6 months old three meals a day should be enough. Variety is still essential, but it is equally important not to overload the stomach. If the kitten does not finish all its food readily, then give it less next time. Clean water should always be available.

Between 9 and 12 months old your cat is an adult – some breeds mature before others. With the exception of invalids, stud cats and nursing queens (see Chapters 3 and 5) your cat now requires two good meals a day. Some cats do quite well on one meal a day, but these usually live in the country, where they can find extra food themselves. I like to give two meals, one in the morning and the other in the evening, with perhaps a saucer of milk at midday if the cat appears to want it.

Regular meals are most important if the cat's digestion is not to suffer. Make the times to suit yourself, but keep to them as far as possible. My own cat is fed at 8 am and then again about 5 pm. Where a cat is difficult to get in at night, however, it is often a good idea to make the last meal later. You will find that it comes in readily for its food.

Of course you will never in any circumstances turn your cat out at night. It is strange that many people who would never dream of putting out a dog at night will cheerfully put the cat out, even in the worst weather. Apart from the fact that cold and rain are a cat's worst enemies, there is always the fear that your cat may be stolen or pick up a disease from strays. It is also at night that your cat is most useful in the house, for it is then that the mice come out.

But back to the question of food. Appetites vary, so it is difficult to say just how much your cat will need. But of one thing you may be certain: a healthy cat has a good appetite and it may require more food than the average person realises. As a very general guide give 4 to 6 ounces of flesh food daily; divide this into the two equal portions and add brown bread scraps, or tinned cereal food, or a little vegetable if the cat will eat it, or any suitable tit-bits from your own table. Do *not* give potato or white bread.

If possible get your cat to eat raw meat. If it is fussy (or perhaps spoilt!), like mine, then you will have to cook its meat. Lean beef is the best meat you can give a cat. It is sustaining and a wonderful conditioner. Most cats are fond of horseflesh, which is also nourishing and less expensive. But quality varies, so do be sure to get the best. My cat enjoys ox cheek; some cats favour whale-meat. You will soon find out what your own pet prefers.

Lightly-boiled liver is very good for cats and should be fed once or twice a week, not more. Lights are economical but have not much food value. Nevertheless, if well stewed, these can be fed occasionally for a change. Rabbit will almost always be appreciated, but cook it and remove the bones.

Most cats like fish, and almost any kind of fresh fish can be given. It should be boiled until it comes away easily from the bone. Never give salted fish to cats and do *not* give white fish too often. Contrary to general opinion, fish is not nearly as good for cats as meat, and too much of it can cause skin disease.

But just as too much white fish is harmful, tinned fish, such as sardines or pilchards, is excellent. The oil is particularly beneficial, for this will help to remove any loose hairs which your pet swallows in the process of washing itself. It is very important that these hairs should be removed. If allowed to collect in the cat's stomach they form into a matted ball, which can be very dangerous, even fatal. Persian cats are especially susceptible to Hair-ball.

Your cat will, of course, have its own drinking-bowl and feeding-dishes, and these should be kept scrupulously clean. Nowadays all kinds of 'fancy tableware' can be bought for cats, including elaborate pottery dishes with the cat's name engraved on them, and coloured plastic bowls. Unless expense is no object I would prefer to spend the money on good food for my cat. All that is really necessary in the way of crockery is an enamel dish (a saucer for kittens), and an earthenware bowl with a flat base for water. See that the dishes are not chipped, however, or the broken pieces may become the breeding-places for germs.

Before leaving the subject of food, do not forget the proprietary cat foods. Those made by reputable manufacturers are perfectly satisfactory. It is important to realise, however, that there are two types of canned food, so always follow the directions carefully. If you feed a can of high protein meat or fish, for example, you will need to add some cereal. If, on the other hand, you feed a 'complete meal', no additions will be required. Cereal cat foods are equally useful, either for mixing with fresh meat, or as an additional meal – in this case they only need moistening with warm milk or warm water flavoured by Marmite or Yeastrel. All these cat foods and cereal foods can be obtained from pet stores, grocers and chemists. Almost all have vitamins and minerals added.

Finally, never leave uneaten food down for long periods. In the hot weather this is especially dangerous, because it encourages flies.

Although your cat may or may not like vegetables, it will certainly eat grass, its natural medicine. Grass removes all kinds of impurities from the cat's stomach and also induces it to vomit loose fur. You have only to think of the roughness of a cat's tongue to realise how much fur can be swept into the stomach as it washes itself. And, as mentioned previously, this must not be allowed to pass into the intestines.

Where there is a garden, your cat should be able to get all the grass it needs. Otherwise write to the Cats' Protection League, 29 Church Street, Slough, Bucks, for a packet of cat grass seed – Cocks-foot (*Dactylis Glomerata*), to give it the proper name. You will be sent sufficient seed for several pots of grass with full instructions how to grow it. There is no charge for this service, but naturally a stamp to cover postage is appreciated.

Cats keep themselves beautifully clean, the tongue acting as a brush. Nevertheless, your pet cannot be expected to do everything that is required of it, and you will be surprised what a little help on the owner's part will do. This particularly applies to Long-haired cats. If a Persian cat is not groomed daily its lovely, long, silky fur becomes matted and unsightly. If such neglect continues over a long period it may become impossible to comb the tangles out. You would then have to take the cat to a vet, who may even need to put it under an anaesthetic.

If started young enough, most cats love their daily toilet. My cat purrs all the time he is being brushed and never in the least resents my attention. He does not mind my wiping round his eyes with cottonwool, or my occasional treatment to his ears. These are jobs that not even the cleanest cat could manage for itself. Of course, there are just a few cats which are not so co-operative. If yours happens to be one of these, try grooming it before a meal. Do this at a regular time, and you may soon find that your pet is kindlier disposed towards its beauty treatment.

You will need a medium-stiff brush for grooming, obtainable from pet shops or pet-accessory departments of London and Provincial stores. A bristle brush is best for Long-haired cats and a rubber brush for Short-hairs. You will also need a metal comb – almost any type will do as long as the teeth are not too sharp pointed. A fine-toothed flea-comb is also useful.

A wooden bench or table is the best place to groom a cat. If your cat is a Long-haired type, then you should brush it in short, upward strokes, from the tail towards the head. By brushing in this way (in the reverse direction) you get right down to the roots of the fur and do much to prevent the formation of tangles. If you should happen to find a knot or two, these can usually be loosened with the blunt end of a knitting-needle.

Next take your comb, and, holding the cat firmly but gently, comb the hair on the tummy, chest, tail, face surfacings and underneath the tail and legs. Finally, comb along the back and sides, working from the roots of the fur to the tips in the direction of the hair-growth.

The coat should stand away from the body. The ruff (or frill), which is one of the Persian cat's chief attractions, should be brushed up and then combed outwards so that it forms a frame for the face.

All Long-haired cats are groomed in the way just described except the Tabby. The reason is that this cat's markings are its chief beauty. Therefore the fur of the Tabby should be brushed towards the body, not away from it.

A Short-haired cat is much easier to groom. Place the cat on the bench, comb firmly from head to tail and then follow by brushing. Most Short-haired cats love the friction of a rubber brush. It is also excellent for removing loose hairs. Finish off with plenty of hand-grooming – cats are fond of being stroked, and it gives their coats a wonderful sheen. If you are going to show your cat, then finish off with a silk pad or a piece of chamois leather.

After grooming, very gently wipe round the inner corners of your cat's eyes. Do this with cottonwool which you have first dampened with warm water. Use a fresh piece of cottonwool for each eye, and then carefully wipe away any surplus moisture with dry cottonwool.

Provided your pet's ears have been given attention from kittenhood they should only need a weekly treatment. The simplest way of doing this is to dip a wad of cottonwool into boracic lotion, or olive oil, and then gently wipe round the inside of the cat's ear. This will remove all traces of dirt as well as preventing canker, which is most painful for the cat and often difficult to cure. Do not drench the cottonwool, just moisten it.

After treatment, wipe the ears carefully with dry cottonwool and dust in a little Boracic powder or canker powder.

Cats do not welcome a bath, and it is rarely necessary to give one. Nevertheless, a light-coloured cat should have a weekly powder treatment to prevent grease from developing in the coat. Use any of the various proprietary grooming powders. Sprinkle it over the fur and work in with the hands. Do not forget the cat's underparts, also the face and round the ears. Be careful, of course, not to get powder into the cat's eyes. Finish off by brushing and combing in the usual way.

Light-coloured cats sometimes get stains on their tails. If powder and brushing do not remove these, then you will have to wash the tail. Use a pure, soft soap, and warm water to which a little borax has been added. Dry and dust with cleaning powder as just described.

But if you are going to show your cat you may need to bath it. Or a chimney adventure may prove a similar excuse. You will require a fairly deep bowl to stand the cat in, and a good veterinary shampoo. It takes two people to bath an adult cat successfully, so have someone to hold it for you.

Make sure the water is not too hot by testing with your elbow. Stand the cat in the bowl so that the water just reaches to its stomach. Wash your pet's coat, then its legs and tail. Rinse thoroughly and then, very gently, wash the head and face, taking great care not to get any soap near the cat's eyes. Squeeze the water out of the coat and dry with warm towels. Do not on any account let your pet out after bathing. If the weather is cold try to persuade it to sit by the fire for an hour or so. This is also an occasion for a drink of warm milk.

For a Short-haired cat a bran bath is usually the better proposition. Heat the bran in the oven until it can be handled comfortably and rub it well into the cat's fur. Brush out and then apply more bran. Continue in this way until the cat is clean.

If you groom your cat regularly as suggested it should rarely, if ever, be necessary to resort to insect powders. Most cats will pick up an odd flea in warm weather, but this is soon disposed of by combing the coat with a solution of Milton or Dettol. Use a fine-toothed steel comb for this purpose.

Of course your cat will sharpen its claws, although the action would be better described as 'stretching'. Unlike a dog, the cat never walks with its claws protruding, therefore they do not wear down. But although it is quite natural (and beneficial) for the cat to stretch its claws, you do not want it doing so on your furniture. Given a garden, most cats will keep their nails in good condition by clawing at the trees. Where a cat is confined indoors, however, it should be given a scratching-post. This should be high enough for a large cat to stretch its full length while clawing at it, and heavy enough that it cannot be knocked over. It is best made of wood and covered with hessian. If you wish to be really enterprising you can put some catnip between the post and the hessian before covering. Catnip is a tonic herb, and cats adore it.

Should you prefer, you can buy a scratching post from almost any pet shop.

Should you cut a cat's claws? Normally this is unnecessary. Some cats, however, especially the Siamese, have extremely long claws which can do endless mischief unless slightly shortened. To trim a cat's nails is very easy. You can do it with ordinary nail scissors, but do make sure they are really sharp, and only remove the merest points. If you cut further you may split and damage the nails. You might find it easier to buy a pair of circular nail-clippers. These are made specially for cutting the nails of cats and small dogs, and are obtainable at pet stores.

Never allow anyone to persuade you to have your cat de-clawed. This entails removal of the claws by surgery, and is really a very cruel thing to do. A cat needs his claws for jumping and climbing and also for self-defence when necessary. Many British vets rightly refuse to do this operation.

Kittens, like children, love a toy to play with. But never give fluffy wool or rubber balls. In fact, do not give anything which might flake off easily. The pieces could be very dangerous if swallowed. I have yet to meet a kitten which is not thrilled at the sight of a toy mouse. Most cats will also amuse themselves for hours with a ping-pong ball suspended on a string.

You can buy toy mice from pet shops or from the Cats' Protection League, 29 Church Street, Slough, Bucks.

And finally, where there are children in the house, do persuade them to think of the cat as a companion, not merely as a plaything. Some cats love to be picked up and petted, others prefer the comfort of a lap only when they are in the mood. No cat likes to be picked up by its middle so that its legs dangle, or to have its fur stroked 'the wrong way'. The best way to lift a cat is to place one hand behind its front legs and the other hand under its hind quarters. In this way the cat is almost in a sitting position and can be lifted very easily without causing it the slightest discomfort.

CHAPTER 3

ILLNESS

CATS ARE hardy little animals, and fortunately they seldom ail. By comparison with many other domestic pets, some illnesses appear to pass them by altogether. My ten-year-old Siamese has only twice seen a vet. The first occasion was for neutering, and the second, much later, for Conjunctivitis. Happily the latter was soon cured.

So do not allow anything I may say in this chapter to deter you from having a cat. Please believe that none of the more serious illnesses is ever likely to attack your pet. The point is that, should it be unfortunate, an owner must be ready to help.

Of course, the only person to prescribe for illness is a qualified vet. Find out when your nearest one holds his surgery, and keep his telephone number handy in case of an emergency. Treatment is also available through the various animal welfare organisations for pet owners who cannot afford the fees of a private vet. If you live in a neighbourhood where there is no clinic or visiting dispensary, you can obtain vouchers from the RSPCA, the Cats' Protection League and similar societies, for free treatment from a vet. Many vets give hours of their time to this invaluable service, so if you can contribute something towards your cat's treatment, it is naturally appreciated. However, there is always the possibility that you may not be able to get a vet immediately. He (or she) may be out on a call, or, if you live in the country, it may take time before he is able to reach you. Meanwhile the cat must not be allowed to die. In cases of emergency it is surprising what pet owners can do to help.

It is a good idea always to have a few remedies at hand. Like humans, a cat is subject to the occasional cough or cold. Or a tummy upset may follow over-eating. Again, your cat may become involved in a fight – even the best-tempered cat would be strange if it allowed feline intruders into its own garden.

How are we to recognise signs of illness? First we must know what to expect of a cat in perfect health. A healthy cat is a bright cat – vitality is apparent in all its movements. It purrs on being fondled, and always welcomes a game. Even the older cat, which may sleep for many hours each day, should take a lively interest in its surroundings. If your cat slinks off into corners, or lies about behind the furniture, watch it. Listlessness is always a danger sign.

So is loss of appetite, or a harsh and staring coat. For a cat to refuse one meal is rarely cause for alarm, provided it is in good condition otherwise. Lack of exercise may be the reason, or the cat may have found itself a meal elsewhere. Again, you may have spoilt your pet – fastidious cats have been known to refuse meat on a day they fancy fish and vice versa. Also, most cats are extremely conventional, and you may introduce a change of diet of which it does not (at first) approve!

But if your cat continually refuses food, look for further symptoms. Does the animal sneeze continually? Does it dribble from the mouth? What about that cough you noticed? Does it gulp when it tries to swallow?

Any of the above indications could mean just a slight cold, which, given common-sense treatment, should pass off in a day or so. On the other hand, they may mean influenza, or even a more serious complaint. If so, this will require professional attention and very careful nursing.

Stomach troubles usually begin with vomiting or diarrhoea. If your cat vomits grass or swallowed hair, do not worry. If the hair was not ejected it might form into a felted mass, which could be very serious indeed. Nor need you alarm yourself because your cat occasionally vomits a much-relished meal – this only means that it has gobbled its food too quickly.

Persistent sickness is, of course, a very different matter; and no time should be lost in getting expert advice. This is particularly important if the vomit is of a frothy nature, or accompanied by other symptoms such as excessive thirst, foul breath, constipation or diarrhoea.

By now we *do* know if a cat is unwell, even if we have not yet diagnosed the specific trouble. Can you take a cat's temperature? If so this will be a great help, because illness is usually accompanied by a rise in temperature. The normal temperature of a cat is 101 to 102 degrees F (about 38 degrees C) according to where it is taken. The most satisfactory place to take it is in the cat's rectum, although it can be taken under the armpit or in the thigh.

You will need an ordinary half-minute thermometer, and you should get someone to hold the cat. Shake the mercury down to 98 degrees, smear the point of the thermometer well with vaseline and very gently insert it into the cat's rectum. Leave it there for about a minute. A temperature of, say, 103 degrees is seldom very serious, but should it be over that, then get professional advice.

Nursing a sick cat is never easy. A cat is not a whiner, and when illness comes it prefers to slink off somewhere to die rather than allow anyone to fuss over it. The patient should, therefore, not be worried by too frequent handling. Nevertheless, it must be kept warm and clean. Also, it must be given its medicines according to instructions.

Never allow a sick cat to lie about in draughty corners or on cold linoleum. Nor should you let it out in the garden, where it may sit about on damp grass and catch more cold. The best place for a sick cat is a warmly lined basket, and this should be raised off the ground and placed well out of draughts. Your pet will also appreciate a hot-water bottle, which should be well-covered and then slipped underneath the top blanket of its basket.

Care during the night is equally as important as during the day – indeed, it is often in the early hours of the morning that attention is most needed. Where there is discharge from the mouth and nose, this should be gently wiped away with cottonwool wrung out in warm water to which a few drops of mild disinfectant such as TCP has been added. A touch of glycerine or warm olive oil rubbed on the nostrils will help to prevent soreness. In cases of diarrhoea the fur and rear parts will also need attention.

Like humans, most cats object to taking medicine. In their case it is understandable, however, because they cannot know we are trying to help them. Whenever possible give a tasteless medicine. In my opinion the homoeopathic and biochemic remedies surpass all others – Aconite, Baptisia or Belladonna for colds, Nux Vomica for constipation and stomach troubles, Arnica for exhaustion or shock, Calendula lotion for dressing wounds, and so on. These homoeopathic medicines are mostly tasteless and can be mixed in with the cat's food. Or, if the cat is declining food, the tablets can be crushed and then slipped on to the cat's tongue, holding the mouth closed until the powder is swallowed. Watch carefully, however, to make sure that it *is* swallowed, for cats are very clever at ejecting medicines when their owners are out of sight. Always be sure to go to a homoeopathic chemist and, unless prescribed otherwise, buy the tablets in the 3X potency.

A good way of dosing liquid medicine is through a plastic medicine dropper. Or you can buy a special medicine spoon from pet shops. It has a curved spout, similiar to a teapot spout, which is placed just inside the cat's lips so that it dribbles the liquid through its teeth. In this way the cat never gets sufficient medicine in its mouth so that it can froth it back at you, which usually happens when the physic is given from an ordinary spoon. Nor is there any danger of the cat choking.

Much gentle coaxing is often necessary to persuade a sick cat to take food. Never feed a cat forcibly until everything you can think of to tempt the appetite has been tried. The smallest amount of food taken voluntarily will do more good than any given by artificial means. Invalid diet includes such delicacies as Brand's Essence, which is very nourishing and easily digested, steamed fish, grilled chicken's liver, meat jelly, Benger's food, Sherley's Lactol with a raw egg beaten into it, or an egg which you have left in warm water for about a minute before removing from its shell. The latter is very strengthening, and many cats will eat it when refusing all other food.

Where the stomach is affected try your cat with Slippery Elm Food. This is the name given to the bark of the Red Elm and Moose Elm of Canada and America because it so aptly describes its peculiar nature. This tree-bark food has amazing healing properties and is very easy to digest. It is obtainable from health food stores and herbalists, and should be mixed with milk or water.

Suppose all your efforts fail? Then some form of liquid nourishment should be given from a spoon. You could try a little barley-water or milk and barley-water; glucose and water, or glucose and milk. Other suggestions include raw meat juice or diluted yeast extract, Sherley's Lactol, raw meat juice mixed with Sherley's Lactol, any of the baby milk foods, in fact anything of a light and nourishing nature that the cat will take.

A sick cat cannot digest much food at once, so you will need to feed at frequent intervals – say, every hour or two. Feed with a smooth plastic teaspoon, which is very easily inserted between the cat's teeth at the side of the mouth. Gently raise the cat's head with your left hand and do the feeding with your right hand. Never force the cat's mouth open, or it will try to struggle, and be sure to insert the spoon at the side of the mouth so that the fluid is poured in very slowly. If the food is still rejected, or frothed back at you, then try the plastic dropper, or special spoon as suggested for dosing medicine.

Except when suffering from gastritis, a sick cat should always be allowed water. Even when refusing all other food, some cats will lap water, and this will keep them alive for a considerable time. Often, however, after a few laps of water a cat will voluntarily eat a little food.

As soon as the cat's strength returns, try to tempt it with more solid food. Do not overload the stomach, but coax your pet with small quantities at a time. Raw or cooked beef, grilled kidney, cooked rabbit, steamed fish, lightly-boiled liver, boiled sheep's brains, boiled tripe, sardines – any of these could be given in alternation.

For a tonic you cannot do better than give yeast. This contains vitamin B, which helps the cat to digest its food and generally restores condition. It can be given in powdered form, either over the food or in milk, or in tablet form (Phillips' Kit-zyme or Sherley's), 2 or 3 tablets daily for adult cats and half a tablet daily for tiny kittens.

Early diagnosis is half the battle in almost any feline illness, so I am now going to give some details of ailments which could attack your cat. In the case of minor illnesses, accident and less serious forms of skin trouble, you will find suggestions for home treatment. Where more serious illnesses are concerned you should be guided only by the veterinary surgeon, and any suggestions here are made with the intention of helping until he (or she) arrives.

Ear, Nose and Throat

Ear Canker

Your cat continually scratches behind the ear, shakes its head, keeps one ear lower than the other, rubs it against the furniture – all or any of these signs indicate canker. Often the ear is inflamed, the outer edge may be crusted. Examination of the inside of the ear will almost certainly reveal a brownish discharge, and if you were to look at this under a magnifying glass, tiny insects could be seen moving about. It is these ear mites which cause the irritation.

Ear canker is not difficult to cure provided it is taken in the early stages. Pour a little warm olive oil into the cat's ear and leave it there for about 10 minutes. Meanwhile you should gently massage the base of the ear to make sure that the oil reaches all the crevices. Now wipe the ear as clean as possible with dry cottonwool, but do this very gently or you may cause the ear to bleed. Repeat the treatment daily for several days until the trouble clears up.

If it doesn't clear up, take your cat to the vet, who will examine the ear with an auroscope and prescribe the appropriate treatment.

Haematoma – Injury to the Ear-flap

A cat often injures the flap of its ear after fighting. Again, such an injury may occur from scratching the ear in an attempt to relieve canker. Whatever the cause, if blood is allowed to form between the layers of the skin, a swelling may appear on the ear-flap. Never neglect a Haematoma. If the swelling is not removed the cat develops a crumpled, or 'cauliflower' ear, which is very disfiguring.

Home cure depends entirely upon very early treatment. Try bathing with warm garlic lotion (two or three garlic tablets crushed into warm water), and give two garlic tablets internally for several days until the trouble clears up. Garlic can be obtained from health-food stores and herbalists. Containing Acrolein, nature's strongest disinfectant, it is a wonderful healing agent, destroying bacteria and purifying the bloodstream.

If the swelling does not subside, however, then call a vet who will remove it. He will also prescribe further treatment for healing the wound.

Nasal Catarrh

The common cold affects a cat in much the same way as it does a human. The animal sneezes frequently and there is a persistent discharge from the nose and eyes. Provided there is no temperature and the cat has a good appetite, the trouble should soon clear up. Keep your pet warm, in one room for preference, but not in a stuffy atmosphere. Give homoeopathic Aconite at the first sneeze – two tablets in the 3X potency. Repeat the dose several times a day, either crushing the tablets into a little warm milk, or slipping the powder on to the back of the cat's tongue and keeping its mouth closed until swallowed. Kittens should have one tablet per dose.

Should the cold already have developed, then give Baptisia instead of Aconite. This should be given in the same dosage and potency (3X). Homoeopathic Aconite is a wonderful remedy, but it must be taken in the very early stages of the illness, otherwise Baptisia often acts best. Yeast tablets are also helpful.

Unless its throat is sore, the cat will probably be able to eat meat, and this is best given raw, because it is more strengthening. Should it be necessary to tempt the appetite, then any of the invalid foods mentioned earlier can be tried.

Make sure, however, that you do not confuse the symptoms of a slight cold with those of influenza, or an even more serious complaint. If there is much coughing, or dribbling from the mouth, then get veterinary advice. In the meanwhile give the homoeopathic remedies suggested, for these will help to keep the temperature down. If you have other cats be sure to isolate the patient. A cat will not pass on its cold to you, but it will soon do so to any feline companions.

Ozoena, or Snuffles

A chronic form of catarrh which sometimes occurs after a bad cold or distemper. As the name implies, the cat sneezes, sniffs and snorts almost continuously. In doing so it discharges a thick, yellow mucus from the nostrils.

This is not a dangerous complaint, but, of course, it is very tiresome both for the cat and owner. It is also annoying, because the cure for one cat is not by any means the same as that for another. Nowadays, however, there are powerful antibiotics which are found to give relief. So do get veterinary advice as soon as possible.

Inflammation of the Throat

Almost the worst form a cold can take is when it affects the throat. The cat gulps continuously, and usually refuses food owing to the difficulty in swallowing. The glands of the neck may be swollen – sometimes there is a cough or slight temperature.

Keep the cat in a warm, but well-ventilated, room. Feed every two hours or so with warm milk into which you have crushed a homoeopathic Belladonna tablet (3X potency). You may have to feed from a spoon as described earlier.

You could also try pouring a teaspoonful of diluted Permanganate of Potash – 10 drops to a tumblerful of warm water – into the cat's mouth several times a day. Do not worry if the cat swallows it for Permanganate is not poisonous. To do any good, however, it must go back as far as possible so that it reaches the affected part of the throat.

If there is no improvement call the vet, who may paint the throat or prescribe Penicillin injections. Probably he will also suggest a tonic, otherwise give a course of yeast tablets crushed over the food.

Choking

A cat which is allowed fish, rabbit or other poultry bones, may get them lodged in its throat. Symptoms are frequent coughing, gulping or vomiting. Usually the cat refuses food and acts as if the throat were sore.

Wrap your pet in a thick rug (or blanket) so that its head remains outside. Get someone to hold the cat while you open its mouth and remove the bone. For this you will need a pair of forceps – never try to remove a bone from an animal's throat with your fingers, or you may get bitten. If there is the slightest difficulty call the vet.

Eye Troubles

Cold in the Eye

As with humans, a cold in the eye is indicated by inflammation or a watery discharge. Bathe the eye with warm boracic lotion – a teaspoonful of crystals to a pint of water. Dry carefully, then squeeze a very little golden eye ointment, or homoeopathic Calendula ointment, between the lids. If the trouble is just a slight chill it should soon clear up.

Make sure, however, that the cat is not sickening for Distemper, which may begin with swollen eyes and a thick discharge. If the cat is off its food, or running a temperature, call the vet immediately. Suggestions will be given for emergency treatment of Distemper a little later.

Protrusion of the Third Eyelid

At the inner corner of the cat's eye is a membrane, or third eyelid, which is commonly known as the 'haw'. Normally this is not noticed because it remains concealed by the lower eyelid. Nevertheless, a cat can draw it across its eye at will, and it is in fact Nature's method of protecting the eye from dust and other foreign matter.

When this 'haw' (third eyelid) suddenly protrudes and remains noticeable for any length of time, then there is a reason. It may happen if the cat has a cold, a tummy upset, or is temporarily run down. Sometimes it appears in cases of anaemia. It may even indicate some more serious eye-trouble such as Conjunctivitis. It could also be a symptom of worms.

Bathe as suggested for a cold, but if the haw remains over the front of the eye for more than a day or so, then veterinary advice should be obtained. A tonic will undoubtedly clear up the trouble, but this must be given under the vet's instructions, because first it is necessary to locate the cause.

Conjunctivitis

Unfortunately this distressing eye-complaint is fairly common in cats and kittens. Symptoms are inflammation and swelling of the eyes, accompanied by a watery, or sticky, discharge. The lids may be gummed together, and the cat often objects to light. It will often rub its paw over the affected eye in an attempt to relieve the irritation and soreness. One or both eyes may be affected.

Bathe constantly with warm boracic lotion. Dry very gently with cottonwool, and squeeze a little golden eye ointment or homoeopathic Calendula ointment between the lids. If there is no improvement take your cat to the vet who will probably prescribe antibiotic drops or ointment.

Ulcerated, or Blue Eye

Occasionally an ulcer develops near the cornea of a cat's eye which may be due to fighting, or the after-effects of Distemper. The eye has a bluish, opaque appearance, and there is a watery discharge. As with Conjunctivitis, the eyelids may be semi-closed and usually the cat objects to the strong light. Get the vet as soon as possible. If this condition is neglected the cat may lose its sight.

Mouth, Teeth and Gums

Kittens rarely have trouble with their baby teeth, but often do so in cutting their second teeth. This may occur between the ages of 4 and 7 months, symptoms being very sore gums, so that the kitten finds difficulty in eating. Often there is foul breath, and occasionally teething fits.

Remove any loose milk-teeth, which usually come out quite easily with tooth forceps. Bathe the gums with warm water to which has been added a few drops of Permanganate of Potash or TCP. Continue this treatment daily until the trouble clears up.

A little medicinal paraffin or olive oil should be given to keep the bowels normal. Try olive oil for preference because cats usually lap this readily. Keep the kitten off meat, though steamed or boiled fish can be given. Boiled tripe is also easily digested.

Where fits occur, send for the vet immediately. Do *not* try to prescribe yourself. If you see the kitten foaming or twitching at the mouth, perhaps kicking out wildly or crying and knocking against the furniture, any of these symptoms may mean a fit. Do not get alarmed; if your pet is shut in a dark hamper it will soon recover. But throw a blanket over it first so that you can pick it up in safety. If the kitten quietens down before the vet arrives, you can let it out of the basket. Nevertheless, it should have a medical examination all the same.

Tartar on the Teeth

If cats are given too much sweet or sloppy food, tartar collects on the teeth, which can cause all kinds of trouble. If you notice your cat eating very slowly, or dribbling from the mouth, examine its teeth carefully. Usually there is foul breath, inflamed and swollen gums, often an abscess and much toothache. In severe cases the cat may paw its mouth, shake its head or rub its head against the furniture in an attempt to ease the pain. Call the vet, who will remove the tartar and, if necessary, any affected teeth. But cats which are fed on meat, and are occasionally given a non-splinter bone to gnaw, are rarely troubled with tartar, especially if the teeth are attended to from time to time.

A good idea is to wipe over the teeth with cottonwool which you have first moistened with a weak solution of Permanganate of Potash – 10 drops to a tumblerful of warm water.

Digestive Ailments

Biliousness

As mentioned earlier, when a cat vomits undigested food there is rarely cause for alarm. Kittens are notorious for gobbling their meals too quickly. Persistent sickness after food, however, usually means a stomach disorder, especially if accompanied by unusual thirst, offensive breath, much yawning, constipation or diarrhoea.

Withhold all food for twenty-four hours; even then, feed only very small quantities at a time. If milk is given, add a few drops of lime-water. The best type of food is minced raw meat, or steamed or lightly boiled fish. Homoeopathic Nux Vomica tablets (3X potency) should prove beneficial. One or two such tablets should be crushed in the food for an adult cat, or half a tablet for a young kitten.

If frothy liquid or yellow mucus is vomited, send for the vet immediately, for this may be a symptom of a more serious illness.

Hair-ball

As the name implies, Hair-ball is the accumulation of loose hairs which have been pulled out and swallowed when the cat washes itself. Long-haired cats are far more likely to suffer from Hair-ball than the short-haired breeds, although all cats are subject to it when they shed their coats, during the spring and autumn.

Symptoms of Hair-ball are a dry cough, a distended stomach and the vomiting of hair and saliva. If the hair-ball is allowed to reach the intestines, the cat may become very ill indeed, and sometimes surgery is necessary for removal.

So always remember that there is never any real reason to allow hair in the stomach to accumulate. Much can be done in the way of prevention by regular grooming, as described in Chapter 2, and by making sure your pet always has access to grass. In addition, give your cat a teaspoonful of olive oil weekly, or see that it gets oily food, such as sardines.

Once Hair-ball has developed, if it has not reached the intestines it can often be dislodged with plenty of olive oil. A teaspoonful night and morning can be given to an adult cat with perfect safety. The idea is to lubricate the stomach well so that it gradually loosens the tangled hairs.

Diarrhoea

Unfortunately this complaint is fairly common in cats. Nor is it always easy to cure, because the causes are so numerous. Persistent diarrhoea should never be neglected. If home treatment fails to effect any improvement within a reasonable time, then veterinary advice should be obtained.

Some kittens suffer from diarrhoea after they have been weaned, or as a result of indigestion or over-eating. Often it is a symptom of a more serious illness, such as Distemper. Or it can be the result of a liver disease, in which case the motions are grey or almost white. Occasionally old cats suffer from chronic diarrhoea. In kittens the trouble is often due to worms.

Provided the diarrhoea is not serious, it can usually be stopped with Carbonate of Bismuth – as much as will cover a new penny piece to be mixed with the food three times a day. If you prefer, you can use powdered Kaolin. This answers the same purpose. After a few days discontinue treatment and watch results. If there is a recurrence, consult your vet. He will diagnose the cause and prescribe accordingly.

If the trouble is due to worms, segments may be passed with the cat's motions or it may vomit some of them up. Possibly there will also be other symptoms. Often the coat is harsh and staring, instead of glossy; or the cat gets painfully thin in spite of a ravenous appetite. Here again you should consult your vet, because only cats in good health should be wormed. Also it is important to be sure whether you are treating round-worms or tape-worms, because a medicine which cures one kind may not be successful with the other.

To keep a cat *free* from worms, however, I would recommend oil or garlic. This is best given in capsule form, one capsule two or three times a week. Absolutely tasteless, the pill is just slipped on to the back of the cat's tongue, and its mouth held closed until swallowed.

But whether the diarrhoea is due to worms or other causes, the diet must be carefully studied. Cut out all milky food and replace with small meals of raw, minced meat. Beef should be given for preference. In liver cases well-boiled rice is excellent, and this is particularly appreciated if mixed with an equal quantity of lightly-boiled fish. Other suggestions which often prove useful include arrowroot or cornflour made with water, barley-water, or the white of an egg beaten up with glucose and water.

Constipation

Cats which are fed correctly and allowed plenty of exercise should not become constipated. Sometimes, however, the trouble may occur as a result of Hair-ball. Occasionally it follows an attack of diarrhoea. It can also be a symptom of the very serious complaint, Feline Infectious Enteritis, of which more will be said later.

Assuming that faulty diet or lack of exercise is the cause, crush two tablets of homoeopathic Nux Vomica (3X) into a knob of butter and give it to the cat. Kittens of, say, four months old should be given one tablet; younger kittens half a tablet.

Never give strong aperients to cats except under veterinary guidance. In obstinate cases, however, pure olive oil, medicinal paraffin oil or milk of magnesia are perfectly safe. About a teaspoonful is usually sufficient for an adult cat.

Avoid all starchy foods, but a good meal of lightly-boiled liver is excellent. Oily foods such as sardines and pilchards also have a laxative effect. In some cases a saucer of milk answers the same purpose.

When the trouble clears up a course of yeast tablets should help to keep your pet in good condition.

Gastritis

In its simple form Gastritis is not uncommon and need cause no alarm. However, it is very important that you should diagnose the symptoms correctly, because they are similar to those of Feline Infectious Enteritis, the most deadly of cat illnesses.

Gastritis, or inflammation of the stomach, is caused by a chill. Or it may be the result of long-standing indigestion. Again, it can occur from eating poultry bones or putrid meat, or accompany Distemper.

Symptoms are great thirst and severe vomiting. Usually, however, there is only a slight rise in temperature.

Assuming that the cat is suffering from only a mild form of

Gastritis, withhold all normal food for several hours. Nor should the cat have access to drinking-water. Instead, give the white of an egg mixed with a tablespoonful of water and half a teaspoonful of brandy. Feed a teaspoonful of this mixture at hourly intervals until the sickness stops.

You could also give five grains of Bismuth on the back of the tongue. Do not give this more than twice, however, and then only at two-hourly intervals. If there is no improvement call the vet.

After an attack of Gastritis do not be in too much of a hurry to put the cat back on to solid food. For a day or two give steamed fish instead of meat. Then give one of the more easily-digested meats, such as mutton.

Inflammation of the Bladder

This painful complaint is also known as Cystitis. It affects male cats, especially neuters, and is caused by gravel in the bladder which blocks the urinary passage. Symptoms are lassitude, increased temperature, refusal to take food and a constant straining to pass water, which is sometimes tinged with blood. Often a cat which is perfectly clean in its habits will become dirty and refuse to use its tray. Frequently a cat will cry out while straining, and this sign may be taken for constipation. If the cat's abdomen is pressed between the fingers, however, a swelling will often be felt.

Usually the trouble clears up satisfactorily provided you get the vet in time. This is *not* a case for home treatment. Meanwhile you should keep the cat warm and persuade it to drink as much as possible. Barley-water is particularly beneficial if the cat will take it. A good idea is to put a tablespoonful of pearl barley in a muslin bag and slip this in the water when you are boiling fish. When the fish is cooked, strain off the liquor and allow to cool. The fishy flavour will probably tempt the cat to drink.

Adhere strictly to the vet's advice regarding diet. To prevent a recurrence give Bicarbonate of Potash, enough to cover a new penny piece, mixed with the food or milk, two or three times a day. This should be continued over a fairly long period. Take the cat off meat, but steamed or boiled fish can be given. The milk should always be warmed.

PARASITES

Fleas

Most cats will pick up an occasional flea in warm weather. Fortunately, however, this is soon disposed of by combing the coat with a fine-toothed steel comb which has been dipped into a solution of Milton or Dettol.

The flea-infested cat is a more serious problem. If you follow the suggestions for grooming which were given in Chapter 2 your cat should never become flea-ridden. But, of course, you may adopt a stray cat, when one of your first jobs will be to rid it of vermin.

Many of the fleas will hop off, so your best place to treat the cat is in the garden or on a balcony. Otherwise use the kitchen table, but be sure to cover it with plenty of newspaper.

The best type of insect powder is one containing Pyrethrum or Derris, as these are perfectly safe if the cat licks its coat. Except under veterinary guidance, never use DDT on a cat. This is perfectly harmless normally, but it may prove lethal if the cat licks itself. Sherley's insect powder, Boots' insect powder or Cooper, MacDougall's 'Pulvex' (now made without DDT) can all be recommended.

Sprinkle the powder well into the cat's fur. But first brush its fur the wrong way to ensure the powder getting right down to the skin. Do not forget the cat's neck or under the legs, for fleas often favour these parts. The tail should also be treated.

Leave the powder in the fur for about 15 minutes. Now brush the fur gently the *right* way to remove both powder and fleas. Of course, you will be very careful of the cat's eyes.

An even better idea is to put the cat in a linen bag, after rubbing the powder well into its coat. The bag should have a draw-string top so that only the cat's head protrudes. Hold your pet in this position for 10 or 15 minutes, and then let it free. You will be surprised at the number of fleas that remain in the bag!

If the cat is badly infested one treatment will not be enough, so repeat at least twice weekly for a short time. It might then be a good idea to put an insecticidal collar on your cat. These are obtainable from most pet shops, and are claimed to protect the animal from fleas for up to two months, or more. Always remember that fleas, besides being irritating to the cat, are often responsible for the more serious skin complaints as well as anaemia and tapeworm.

Be sure to keep the cat's bedding clean. Baskets should be scrubbed with strong soda from time to time, then rinsed with warm water and Dettol, after which they should be left out in the air to dry. If a kitten is in the habit of playing in dusty cupboards, these should be scrubbed out too. Such places are favourite breeding quarters for fleas.

Chicken Fleas

Country cats which wander about near chicken-houses sometimes get these small fleas round the edges of their ears and eyes. These are not the usual type of flea, but attach themselves to the cat's skin. They can usually be removed with tweezers. To relieve the soreness bathe with Garlic lotion (one tablet crushed in warm water), or equal parts of warm water and TCP.

Lice

Cats are not usually troubled with lice unless their coats have been neglected. This particularly applies to the Long-haired breeds, because a dirty, matted coat lends itself to infestation.

Lice are small, greyish-yellow parasites. They move extremely quickly and can be most difficult to dispose of. Indications are a dull and sticky coat with much scratching on the part of the cat.

Derris or Pyrethrum powders can be used, although it is better to bathe in warm water to which a disinfectant such as Milton or Dettol has been added. Another suggestion is to comb the cat with a solution of vinegar and water – one part vinegar to two parts water. This will help to loosen the nits from the coat.

The most effective method, however, is to clip off all the cat's fur on to a newspaper, then burn the paper and clippings. Now sprinkle on your Derris or Pyrethrum powder and work it in with the fingers. This *does* sound very drastic, but it is the only way of getting rid of all the eggs which stick to the cat's fur.

Ticks

Occasionally a country cat will pick up a tick, especially if it has access to fields where sheep have grazed.

A tick is a bloodsucking parasite. It buries its head in an animal's skin, then saps the victim's energy by sucking its blood. At this early stage the tick is hardly noticeable, being so small. Very soon, however, it begins to swell with the cat's blood and becomes much larger. It then assumes a bulbous shape, turning a purplish-blue colour. By now, of course, it is quite easy to distinguish, but often difficult to remove. Unless the head is completely dislodged an abscess might develop.

To make the tick release its hold you should place a drop of turpentine on the point where the head is buried. If you prefer, you can paint round the spot with iodine. Remove the tick with a pair of tweezers and bathe with Garlic lotion or warm water and TCP.

Skin Diseases

Eczema

Eczema is *not* contagious, but it can be very difficult to cure. Even when it appears to have cleared up completely it often breaks out again, especially during warm weather. No one knows what causes Eczema, but it is probably due to a blood disturbance, the result of wrong feeding.

There are two forms of Eczema: dry and moist. With dry Eczema the cat's fur comes away and leaves bare patches. Sometimes these are much larger than a fifty pence piece. In moist Eczema the skin is covered with tiny red, discharging sores.

Each type requires different treatment and the vet will prescribe accordingly. Meanwhile apply a soothing lotion such as Calamine and Zinc. Or, if you cannot get this, try bathing the affected parts with warm Boracic lotion. Dry gently with a soft, clean cloth and dust on Boracic Powder. To prevent your pet from licking the sore places make it a wide collar of stiff cardboard. Place this round the cat's neck and fasten by lacing it up at the join.

A cat suffering from Eczema should not be given milky foods or starch. Try to provide a varied diet which includes raw or cooked meat, boiled fish and rabbit. If a cat has been fed only on fish it is often helpful to change over to meat for a while, and vice versa. Yeast is excellent and has in fact been known to cure without any other treatment. An adult cat could be given up to eight tablets a day in cases of skin trouble. You should also see that the cat drinks plenty of water.

Dandruff

This is a dry form of Eczema, but not so serious. Try rubbing just a touch of olive oil into the cat's skin before brushing. This treatment combined with the correct diet and a course of yeast tablets should soon cure.

Ringworm

This disease is not very common in cats but when it does occur is highly contagious. It can be passed on to human beings and to other animals.

There are various forms of Ringworm, but the type which usually attacks cats is Microsporosis, or Grey, Ringworm.

Early symptoms are hairless spots, or perhaps just roughness of the skin, revealing grey scales rather like tobacco ash. The cat does not scratch and there appears to be no irritation. Isolate your pet and get the vet as soon as possible.

A cat may also pick up Favus, or Honeycomb, Ringworm. This is sometimes contracted from affected mice or from lying in straw previously occupied by diseased cattle. Indications are circular, raised yellow scabs. These usually break out on the cat's face and then spread to other parts of the body, especially the legs and feet.

Both types of Ringworm are usually curable, but a great deal of patience may be required. Also – and this applies especially to the Microsporosis form – the disease spreads very rapidly indeed. Therefore bear in mind its highly contagious nature. Where there are children in the house it might be kinder to have the cat humanely put to sleep.

Mange

This is another highly contagious disease. There are two forms – Sarcoptic and Follicular. Sarcoptic Mange is also known as 'Red Mange', and it is this type which usually attacks cats. Fortunately this kind is easier to cure.

A clean, well-cared-for cat should never get Mange. However, there is always the chance that your cat may be unfortunate enough to pick up this foul disease from a stray.

Mange is caused by a parasite which burrows underneath the skin and sets up intense irritation. The sarcoptic form almost always starts on the head and neck, but if taken early enough it may not spread to the body. Symptoms are repeated scratching by the cat, which is due to the violent irritation. The hair comes off in patches, revealing the skin, which is covered with small pimples. As the cat continues to scratch, these spots bleed and eventually form scabs. The cat goes on clawing itself, and the scabs become scaly. Because there are poisons in the system, the cat is usually very weak and thin. Get veterinary advice as soon as mange is suspected.

You will need to keep the patient isolated and see that it

gets plenty of nourishing (but not starchy) food. Yeast tablets, as suggested for Eczema, can be given. Also add a few drops of halibut-liver oil to the food.

Once your cat is well again, burn all the bedding and disinfect the surroundings thoroughly. If this is not done reinfection will occur.

Accidents

Burns and Scalds

Cats have a wonderful sense of danger and rarely burn themselves. Nevertheless, a cat which is in the habit of warming itself by sitting near the hot plate of an electric cooker may get too near and blister the pads of its feet. Or an inquisitive cat could easily tip up a saucepan of boiling liquid and scald itself.

Treatment always depends on the burn. For just a slight burn a compress of cold, strong tea is usually very effective. For severe burns, caused by fire or heat, cover the affected parts with olive oil or vaseline. Then get the vet.

If a burn is caused by boiling water, a compress of ice-cold water should be applied. This must be done very quickly, however, or the boiling water will burn through the surface of the skin. For shock you should crush a homoeopathic Arnica tablet (3X) into a little warm milk. Homoeopathic Arnica can also be given internally in all cases of bruised muscles, sprains of the joints or fractured bones.

Traps

If you live in the country there is always the danger of your cat getting one of its legs caught in a trap. You will have to step on the springs of the trap. It will then open, and you can pull the cat's foot out. Before you try to free your pet it is advisable to throw a cover over its head, or you may get bitten. If there is an injury get the vet as soon as possible. Meanwhile dose with homoeopathic Arnica as described for burns.

Cuts and Wounds

Cats do not often cut themselves – probably intuition warns them of the danger of broken glass, sharp stones, barbed wire and so on. However, accidents are bound to happen occasionally, and it is as well to be prepared. If the bleeding is profuse it can usually be stopped by swabbing with cold water and then dressing the wound with a solution of Calendula lotion – one teaspoonful to a pint of water. Calendula officinalis is not an antiseptic in the true sense, but germs do not thrive in its presence. It is extremely soothing and a wonderful healer.

If the wound is jagged, as may happen if the cat injures itself on barbed wire, then clip all the hair surrounding it before bathing. If this is not done the wound might turn septic. Should stitching be necessary call the vet.

Punctured wounds – when, for example, the cat is jabbed by a nail – must not be allowed to heal too quickly. If the mouth of the cavity is not kept clean and open until the bottom of the wound has healed, infection may remain below and result in the formation of an abscess. Keep the wound open by syringing it out daily with a solution of Calendula, then pack it lightly with gauze soaked in Calendula lotion, cover with dry gauze and bandage. If you cannot get Calendula lotion (it is only obtainable from a homoeopathic chemist), then use Ferram Phosphate, which is obtainable from health food shops. To prepare a lotion, dissolve ten tablets in half a tumblerful of water, which has been previously boiled and left to cool. Otherwise, you can use a mild disinfectant such as Dettol or TCP, but always keep the Calendula or Ferram Phosphate by you if possible.

Few cats will keep a bandage on, but if you make a little sock of washleather this can be slipped over it. Make sure, of course, that the bandage is not too tight.

Serious Illnesses

Distemper

Perhaps it is customary to think of Distemper in connection with dogs. Unfortunately, this very serious complaint attacks cats too, but in quite a different form. Also, it is worth remembering that while Cat Distemper is very contagious to other cats, and Dog Distemper to other dogs, a cat cannot infect a dog, or vice versa. This is mentioned in case you keep both a cat and dog and one of them has the misfortune to get Distemper.

Cat Distemper – or 'Cat Flu', as it is often called – is a misleading term because there are several forms of the illness. Of these the catarrhal form is the most usual and fortunately the easiest to cure. In fact eighty per cent of the cases make a good recovery. However, it must be understood that other symptoms, usually of an abdominal or bronchial nature, often occur. These can be very difficult to treat, and recovery depends on getting a good vet and carrying out his (or her) instructions.

In the very early stages catarrhal distemper is easily mistaken for an influenza cold, except that there is nearly always a high temperature. Often the illness comes on suddenly – a cat may be quite well in the morning yet sneezing violently in the evening. The sneezing is accompanied by a thick mucus which sometimes changes to a profuse watery discharge. The eyes become inflamed and swollen, and the lids stick together as a result of the discharge. Sometimes there is dribbling and a sore throat. Usually the coat is staring.

Keep the patient warm. Until the vet arrives give homoeopathic Aconite (3X) at very frequent intervals. This will help to keep the fever down. Keep the eyes and nostrils free of mucus by wiping gently with cottonwool wrung out in warm Boracic lotion. Swab out the mouth with diluted TCP.

As a result of the catarrh the cat loses its sense of smell, and therefore usually goes off its food. Do all you can to tempt the appetite with highly-concentrated foods like Brand's

Essence, beef-tea, chicken essence, grilled liver, grilled kidney and so on. Otherwise you will have to keep up the cat's strength by feeding glucose and water (one teaspoonful of glucose to a teacup of water) a little at a time, but at very frequent intervals.

Abdominal Distemper is usually accompanied by much sickness and diarrhoea. Often there is great thirst – the cat may sit over a bowl of water but has not the strength to drink it. As the illness develops, the cat tries to slink away into corners, or lies around in the coolest spot available. The fever is very high.

Keep your pet warm, and try to maintain its strength by feeding glucose-water or thin barley-water. Do your best to persuade it to take small quantities of warm milk, egg and milk or beef essence. The vet will prescribe treatment.

Pharyngeal Distemper is indicated when the cat shows a great fondness for draughts and cold places. There is refusal to take food, and the cat lies stretched out and lifeless. The throat is ulcerated, the gums are sore and inflamed, usually there is dribbling from the mouth. Sometimes there is a cough, sometimes not. The absence of a cough, however, is not necessarily a good sign. Send for the vet immediately. Meanwhile keep the cat warm and try to induce it to take some liquid nourishment.

Never allow a cat out after Distemper until the vet advises that it is safe to do so. Apart from the very serious risk of spreading the disease to other cats in the neighbourhood, your pet might have a relapse. Should that happen the consequences might be fatal.

Distemper attacks cats of all ages, and unfortunately one attack does not confer immunity.

Feline Infectious Enteritis

The oldest-known of cat illnesses, this is also the most fatal. All cats are susceptible, although it usually attacks kittens between three and nine months old. Unfortunately Siamese and Persians appear to be the chief victims.

The illness comes on very suddenly, and death may be only a few hours from the onset of the first symptoms.

Those facts will sound alarming. They are meant to be because, unfortunately, there is still no cure for Feline Infectious Enteritis, or the 'Cat Plague', as it is sometimes called. But – and this is important – you can have your kitten inoculated as a protection against it ever catching the disease. Of course this will *not* guarantee immunity, but personally I have never known a kitten which has been treated with one of the modern vaccines to succumb. If possible, your kitten should have the necessary injections before it is three months old (some vaccines are given at ten weeks, while others can be given even younger), so lose no time in getting the vet's advice. If you buy a pedigree kitten direct from the breeder, he (or she) may have arranged this for you. Even so, booster doses will probably be necessary; your vet will advise you at what intervals they should be given.

Suppose, in spite of all precautions, the illness does attack your pet. Then call the vet immediately, for you have no time to lose. Symptoms are great lassitude, loss of appetite, constant vomiting of a frothy, brown-streaked mucus, chronic constipation and a high temperature. The cat lies on its abdomen with legs stretched out, or sits huddled up without moving. When picked up it cries faintly. The eyes are sunken and the coat is staring.

If you can keep the cat alive for three or four days, then it has a chance of recovery. And if it *does* recover it is immune from this disease for the rest of its life.

Whether it recovers or not, the greatest care must be taken to prevent the illness from spreading to other cats in the neighbourhood. Enteritis germs can be carried on a person's clothes, shoes, even on his stationery. Therefore, in addition to destroying the cat's bedding, baskets, feeding dishes and so on, burn any of your own clothes you wore while looking after it. Do not visit cat shows, and keep away from friends' cats for a time. Finally, however badly you want another kitten, resist the temptation for at least *six* months.

Pneumonia

Fortunately pneumonia in cats is rare. Sometimes, however, it follows a neglected chill. Or it may accompany distemper.

Symptoms are a very high temperature, accompanied by quick and laboured breathing. The cat is listless and off its food. When its chest is touched the cat shows signs of pain.

Call the vet immediately. Meanwhile keep the cat in a warm but well-ventilated room. The sleeping-basket should contain several layers of blanket, and a hot-water bottle should be placed underneath the top blanket. Try to tempt the appetite with liquid foods. A few drops of brandy mixed in warm milk is excellent if you can persuade the cat to drink it.

The vet will probably prescribe antibiotic treatment, and may perhaps suggest that you put the cat into a pneumonia jacket. This is easily made from a piece of flannel, which you should line with several layers of cottonwool. Do not use Thermogene, because cats dislike the smell, and if a cat is worried it will not make much progress. Two holes are cut in the jacket for the cat's front legs. It is then tied along the back with cord or tape.

When the cat recovers, be very careful only to remove the jacket a layer at a time. Otherwise your pet may catch another cold.

Tuberculosis

This is another disease which is, fortunately, rare in cats. When it does occur, however, it is highly contagious to other cats, and there is some risk of it being infectious to humans.

Symptoms are general loss of condition. The cat gets very thin and runs a continuous temperature, although not necessarily a high one. Often one or both eyes become affected, white streaks running across the pupils. Long-standing cases show other symptoms, but the illness should not be allowed to develop that far. Have your cat humanely put to sleep. Tuberculosis in cats is incurable.

CHAPTER 4

SHOWING A CAT

A STRAY tabby kitten was taken to an animal-welfare shelter, from where it found a good home. Its new owner gave it all the kindness and attention it deserved, so that it soon grew into a really beautiful cat. 'Why don't you show it?' asked a friend who bred pedigree cats. She did. It won a first prize!

Never imagine that because your cat is not, say, a Blue Persian or a Siamese, you cannot show it. Many an 'ordinary' cat wins prizes at the cat shows. At a recent all-breed show there were no fewer than 10 classes for household pet cats. In addition to prizes for the best black cat, white cat, ginger cat, tabby cat and so on, many novelty awards were offered. For example, is your cat unusual looking? If so, it might have won a prize. Is it heavy? Does it grin? Has it big eyes, or an unusually long tail?

Prizes were also awarded to the best cat owned by a child, and to the best cat owned by a man. There were many others.

But suppose you do own a Blue Persian or a Siamese, or in fact any of the pedigree varieties. Well, provided it is registered with the Governing Council of the Cat Fancy, it has almost unlimited opportunities. Incidentally, you can also register a non-pedigree cat, which will give it a better opportunity of competing with its more aristocratic rivals. For example, at an all-breed show, as the name implies, classes are organised for every recognised breed of cat, as well as for the lesser-known breeds and cats of mixed breeding. It is in these 'Any Other Variety' classes that the 'ordinary' cat, if attractive enough, often stands a good chance.

Prizes at the championship shows include challenge certificates, silver cups and spoons, rosettes and sums of money, offered in the 'open' (or breed) classes for points of excellence. There are also many special prizes, usually consisting of beautiful trophies, awarded by the various cat clubs for the benefit of their members. Then there are the numerous 'open' specials. These are offered by judges, cat fanciers, manufacturers of cat products and interested members of the public, and may consist of, say, a cat-basket for the best neuter, a cat-blanket for the cat in best condition, a box of chocolates for the cat which is easiest to handle, or a Premium Bond for the best litter of kittens.

By now I hope you may be interested enough to wish to show your cat. Here are some details as to how to go about it. Cat shows are advertised in *Fur and Feather*, the address of which has been given earlier. Or, you can obtain a current list of shows from the Secretary of the Governing Council of the Cat Fancy – Mrs W. Davis, Dovefields, Petworth Road, Witley, Surrey. A stamped, self-addressed envelope should be enclosed, with a 10p postal order.

Your next step is to write to the respective show manager for a schedule.

Most of the important shows are organised by the cat clubs or agricultural societies. Broadly speaking, there are two kinds of cat club: the regional club, which caters for all breeds, and the specialist club, such as the Siamese Cat Club, the Burmese Cat Club and the Blue Persian Cat Society.

All the cat shows are open to anyone who cares to exhibit, but club membership brings considerable advantages, not the least of which is a reduction on entry fees at shows organised by the respective clubs. Many of the clubs also arrange social functions and lectures on cat welfare. In addition, the advice of the club experts is available to members at all times. Annual subscriptions to the cat clubs are very moderate. Fuller particulars may be obtained from the secretaries. A list of cat clubs will be provided by the Secretary of the

Governing Council of the Cat Fancy, whose address is given above, on receipt of 10p plus postage.

So let us say you have received the schedule. With this you will also receive an entry form and a registration form from the Governing Council of the Cat Fancy. The registration form should be filled up first, because no cat or kitten can be exhibited at any show unless it is entered in the Register kept by the Governing Council. The exception to this ruling would be for a cat entered only in the household-pet classes.

On the registration form you will find a space provided for the cat's name, date of birth, name of sire and dam, and also name of grandsire and grandam. Fill these in very carefully, using block letters. If any of the particulars are unknown to you – as may be the case if you have not the cat's pedigree – then you should put 'unknown' in the space provided. The form is then sent to the Receptor, GCCF, Mr R. A. Loveys, 28 Bredon Road, Watchet, Somerset TA23 0AX, together with the registration fee. Mr Loveys will then pass your application to the appropriate registrar. There is one for Long-haired cats, one for Short-haired and three for Siamese.

Suppose you wish to show more than one cat. With the exception of tiny kittens in Litter classes, each cat must be registered separately. Therefore you will need additional forms. These can be obtained, on request, from the respective registrars.

If your cat was already registered when you bought it (most breeders do register their kittens before sale), transfer of ownership must be registered with the Governing Council if the cat is to be exhibited by the new owner. This is quite a simple matter. The form, which is again obtained from the respective registrar, is filled up and signed by the present owner, but it must also bear the signature of the previous owner. If the cat is shared by more than one person, then names of all the owners must be given on the form. There is a nominal fee for transfer of ownership.

Before leaving the subject of registration, remember that if you choose a hyphenated name, this will count as two words.

Only three words are allowed, which includes the breeder's prefix. Most serious breeders do register a prefix with the Governing Council for use in connection with all their cats. For example, my Siamese cat was registered in the name of Silbe Caesar – 'Silbe' being the prefix of the breeder from whom I bought the cat. Whenever I see a reference to any cat with 'Silbe' in front of its name I am able to recognise the breeder. More will be said about prefixes in the chapter on breeding.

Finally, do not register your cat in the name of a living person, celebrated or otherwise. Remember, too, that once a cat is registered you cannot change its official name, although of course there is nothing to prevent you calling your pet by any name you please to suit your own convenience.

Meanwhile you will have studied the schedule. In which classes will you enter your cat? An Open class is one in which cats of any breed, or a variety of breeds, can compete. A Veteran class is for cats of seven years old or over on the day of the show. A Debutant class is for cats or kittens which have never been exhibited at any show held under the Governing Council's rules. A Litter class is for three or more kittens of the same litter between ten weeks and three months old. There are many others. For example, you will find that there is a class for brood queens, another for stud cats, for pairs of kittens, for juniors (cats under two years old) and so on. To compete in any of the kitten classes your pet must be under nine months old. Championship classes, on the other hand, are confined to adult cats of over nine months old.

Entry fees are very moderate. There will also be a small penning fee.

To become a champion, a cat must win three Challenge Certificates, each under a different judge at a different show. Challenge Certificates are granted by the Governing Council of the Cat Fancy at all Championship Shows held under its rules. Two Certificates are usually granted at each show, one for males and the other for females. If your cat wins a first prize in its Open, or breed, class, then it may be awarded a Challenge Certificate. When it has won three of these, the word 'Champion' may be used before the prefix in front of its name.

Neuter cats do not compete for the title of Champion, but for that of 'Premier'. The award, however, is granted on exactly the same conditions. Three Certificates must be won, each on a different occasion and under a different judge.

If your cat is to win a prize it must be in excellent condition. Follow the suggestions for grooming made in Chapter 2. But if you are showing a light-coloured cat, then a little extra attention may be necessary. Bath the cat a few days before the show, so that the fur has time to settle. Brush and comb as described. On the morning of the show dust just a very little powder into the cat's coat. *Then brush all the powder out.* This is most important, because, although it is perfectly legitimate to use powder as part of the show preparation, it must not be found in the cat's coat at the time of judging. If it is, then your cat will be disqualified. A rule of the Governing Council of the Cat Fancy reads:

> A cat shall be disqualified for competition if improperly prepared for exhibition, that is, if any dye, colouring, whitening, or darkening substance, any oils or greasy preparation, and cleaning preparations, or any foreign matter of any description, has been used and remains in the cat's coat during exhibition.

Do not feed your cat within two hours of departure, and, if possible, the last meal before the journey should be lean, raw meat. To give milky food before travelling may mean a soiled hamper. The best drink before a show is clean, fresh water.

If you are unable to take a cat to the show yourself, then you must find someone else to do so. Show managers rightly refuse to accept cats sent unaccompanied. Most of the shows are held in London, or large provincial towns, so transport is almost always available.

You will need a suitable-sized carrying basket to take your cat to the show. This should be high and wide enough to allow your pet complete freedom of movement, but not so large that it rolls about with the movement of the vehicle. Line the inside of the basket with several sheets of newspaper. Cover these with a piece of soft, clean blanket. If the sides of the basket are covered with stiff brown paper, and secured with string, this will safeguard the cat from draughts. Addresses where cat baskets can be obtained were given in Chapter 1.

Before you can take your cat into the show hall it must be examined by one of the veterinary surgeons in attendance. You will find that he (or she) looks at the cat's fur, eyes, ears and throat, checking carefully for signs of parasites, skin disease or any possible infection. Should he find that the cat is unwell, or suffering from any contagious disease, then he has full authority to order its removal. This is only fair to the other competitors. However, most cat owners are scrupulously honest, and there is rarely any trouble in this way.

If there is a large number of exhibits the veterinary examination may take a little time, so do not remove your cat from its basket until called upon to do so. When the time arrives, however, you should be able to unfasten the basket quickly and efficiently. A busy veterinary surgeon may not be very pleased at having to wait while numerous knots of string are being untied. Some of the best types of basket are fastened by two straps.

Once the vet has passed your cat it can be taken into the show hall. There you will find rows of numbered pens (wire cages) arranged on trestle tables. To find your own cat's pen is easy. The number will be the same as that on the tally which the show manager has sent you in advance. If you are showing several cats, then pens and tallies will be allotted to them accordingly.

But do not destroy this tally. You will need it again. Remember it is against your cat's number that the judges make their comments. The names of cats never appear in the judges' books. In fact they do not know to whom any cat belongs until after the judging is over. Therefore, before penning your cat, attach the tally to a piece of *white* tape, ribbon, or thin, rounded elastic which you should then tie round its neck.

Having found the right pen, settle your cat in. Do not put cushions or coloured blankets in the pen. In fact do not decorate the pen in any way until the judging is over. A plain white blanket is permissible, being necessary for the cat's comfort, but it should be folded quite flat. You should also take a sanitary tin with you, although disposable litter trays are sometimes provided. Peat-moss litter is also provided by the show management.

You can give your cat a very quick snack before the judging begins, but put a paper over its blanket while it is eating. Be sure to remove the feeding dish, but leave a little clean drinking water. Drinking bowls are usually provided. Again, however, many exhibitors like to take their own.

Once your cat seems comfortable be prepared to leave it for a few hours. You will have a pass-out ticket, which, like the tally, will bear the number of your cat's pen. This is, of course, a safeguard against anyone claiming the cat in your absence.

At most shows the public is admitted about midday. An exception is the National Cat Club's Show, which is held annually at Olympia, and is open to the public all day. When the public is admitted you can return to the show hall. If there is a large number of entries, however, the judging may not be quite finished. Nevertheless, you can feed your cat, give it a 'petting' if you wish, and make it generally comfortable.

Some exhibitors like to put a piece of transparent polythene over the front of the pen, and this is a good idea because it prevents admirers from touching your cat through the bars, which could be a way of innocently passing on infection. However, this is entirely a matter of preference. Once 'Best in Show' judging is over you are allowed to decorate the cage in any way you please.

Meanwhile you will have looked at the award board to find out if your cat has been successful. If so, cards indicating honours in the different classes will also be displayed on the outside of its pen. Should there be no award cards, do not be discouraged. Cats are judged entirely by their appearance and condition on the day of the show. They cannot possibly look, or feel, their best always.

Unlike the procedure at dog shows, exhibitors of cats are not allowed to handle their pets while the judging is in progress. Each judge is allotted one or more stewards, who remove the cats from their pens and carry them over to a small trolley for the judge's inspection. The stewards then return the cats to their temporary enclosures.

All stewards are great cat lovers, so you can rest assured that your pet will be handled gently and with understanding. Most of the cats are perfectly happy at shows. Many of them appear to revel in the admiration they receive. Others may find the judge's scrutiny rather boring. Nevertheless, they endure it patiently.

But, of course, there are just a few cats which are so nervous that they never acclimatise themselves to show conditions. For them the excitement of the journey and the bustle of the show hall are terrifying. If your cat is of a nervous temperament, then do not show it. A cat may be a beautiful specimen of its breed, but it will not show to advantage if it is frightened of strangers. It may even refuse to allow the stewards to remove it from its pen!

However, let us say that you know your cat is a good specimen and not of nervous disposition. Perhaps it has won prizes at other shows. Well, the judge knows best, so never question his (or her) decision. Being the connoisseurs they are, judges dislike having to withhold awards. On the other hand, most judges will always give you an opinion. Therefore, if you are in any real doubt as to why your cat failed, have a word with the judge. Wait until he has a quiet moment and ask for his advice. You will find that he not only explains your cat's faults, but also offers helpful suggestions for its improvement.

Most shows close about 6 pm, but if you have to travel a long distance you can usually get permission to leave a little earlier.

Get your cat home as soon as possible and give it a meal. Or if the weather is very cold, then give it a drink of warm milk with a few drops of brandy in it. This will help to keep out chills. If you keep other cats, be careful not to go near them until you have bathed and changed your clothes. Such precautions may seem foolish, but if you are to avoid risk of infection you cannot be too careful. The cat which has been to the show should have its fur rubbed over with a solution of mild disinfectant recommended by your vet. And, if possible, do try to keep it away from your other cats for about 14 days.

CHAPTER 5

BREEDING CATS

RAISING KITTENS is a delightful occupation. But, as most breeders will tell you, it needs much patience and perseverance. Beginners do have unexpected good luck, while established breeders may have their failures. Generally speaking, however, experience counts, and, like almost every other occupation, success comes as a result of trial and error.

Do not take up cat-breeding because you think it is lucrative. This is not to say that the hobby cannot be made to pay for itself, or even to show a profit. But to rear good kittens up to a saleable age involves financial outlay.

How should you start? Assuming that you have made up your mind as to the breed you prefer, then buy the best female kitten you can afford. Follow the suggestions made in Chapter 1 for buying a kitten, but when selecting a future brood queen give very careful consideration to pedigree. If possible, try to find a young queen of about six months old. A cat of this age will, of course, be more expensive than a tiny kitten. However, she should be showing her qualities, and may even have achieved some success in the show-pen.

But do not be guided entirely by show points because prize-winners do not always make the best brood queens.

You certainly want a cat which is well above the average standard, but you also want one that comes from healthy parents and is of gentle disposition. When suitably mated, such a cat often produces prize-winning kittens.

Signs of sexual desire in a female cat are known as the oestrum, season or heat. During the spring and summer months this condition occurs fairly frequently, lasting from

THE VAN CAT
FROM TURKEY

RUSSIAN BLUE
SHORT-HAIR

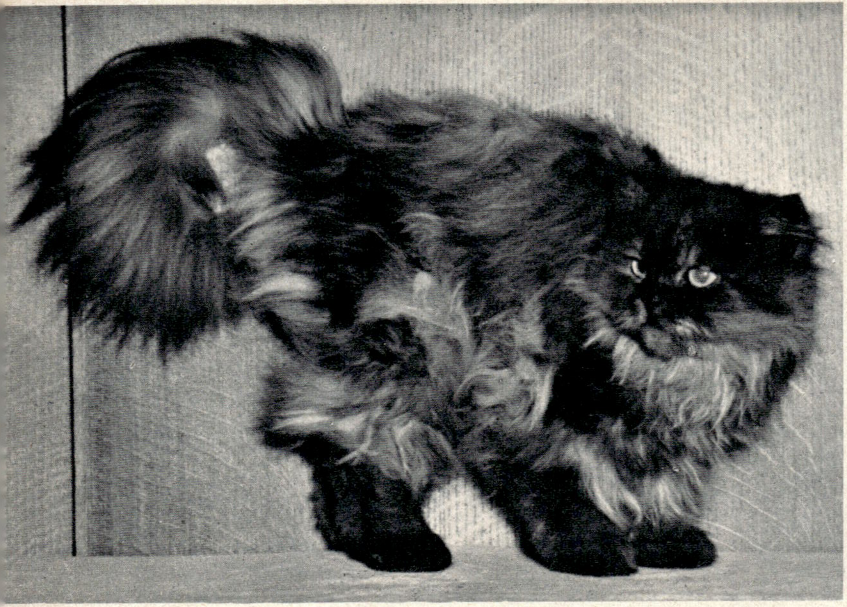
SMOKE LONG-HAIR

RED TABBY

BLUE CREAM LONG-HAIR

TORTOISESHELL LONG-HAIR

CHESTNUT BROWN SHORT-HA

SILVER TABBY SHORT-HAIR

COLOURPOINT LONG-HA

several days to a week, or even longer. Symptoms may include an increase of appetite or refusal to take food. Usually the cat is very restless – she may rub and roll against the furniture, crouch, or scrape the ground with her back legs. Possibly she will overwhelm you with affection.

All this strange behaviour is accompanied by persistent crying to attract the opposite sex. Cat fanciers allude to these love songs as 'calling'.

It is impossible to say when your queen will first come into season, possibly at about seven or eight months old. Some breeds, such as Siamese, often mature very early. Persians, on the other hand, may not show signs of the approaching heat until ten months, or even a year old.

As soon as your cat expresses her desire for a husband, you will have to confine her to the house. Be very careful that she does not escape you. If this happens, naturally she will choose her own suitor, and the result will be a mongrel litter. If your queen does mis-mate, then there are two courses open to you. A vet can give her an injection to avoid the unwanted kittens – this must be done within a few hours to be effective – or you can allow Nature to take its course. If you choose the latter, and perhaps wiser method, do not imagine that the hybrid kittens will make the slightest difference to your queen's future progeny. Rest her for a while and then mate her to a cat of her own breed. If the mating is satisfactory, the result will be pedigree kittens.

Meanwhile, if the little hybrids are not wanted, remove them all, *except one*, immediately. One kitten should be left because unless the milk is taken from the breasts abscesses may form. So keep a male (it is easier to find homes for males), and have the remainder humanely destroyed. Take them to a vet or animal-welfare clinic – do *not* drown them; this is a prolonged and painful death.

Usually it is inadvisable to mate a queen before she is a year old, by which time she is sufficiently mature to bear her kittens easily. Many queens, however, begin calling at seven months old, or even sooner. The Siamese, for example, calls very loudly and persistently, and can usually be mated in the second heat. It might be unwise to deprive her of a family for too long.

How will you find a stud? Many beautiful cats appear regularly at the shows, and preliminary arrangements can always be made with their owners in advance. Advertisements of cats at stud also appear regularly in *Fur and Feather*. Or you can buy an up-to-date list of 'Cats at Stud' from the Secretary of the Governing Council of the Cat Fancy, Dovefields, Petworth Road, Witley, Surrey.

Never choose a stud for your queen merely because there happens to be one in the neighbourhood. Always look for a sire which excels in points where your own cat fails. For example, let us say you are the owner of a lovely Blue Persian. This cat has the type of long, silky, pale-lavender coat which is so much admired. Unfortunately, however, it fails in eye colour, which in this breed should be brilliant orange or deep copper. Your job then is to find a Blue Persian male which really does excel in eye colour, even if his coat is, say, of a little darker blue than that of your own queen. If you can do this, then there is a very good chance of your queen producing at least *some* good-quality kittens in the litter.

One more example: the very popular Seal-Pointed Siamese. This cat should have a short, close-lying coat, the colour of which is rich cream shading to fawn. If your queen is too dark – and this is a fairly common fault – then she may have the most brilliant sapphire-blue eyes, which, of course, are one of the Siamese cat's chief attractions. On the other hand, the desired light coat often means poor eye colour. So here again the choice of stud is obvious. Find a male which excels in points where your own cat is weak.

And never imagine that because a cat is a champion he will necessarily pass on these prize-winning qualities to his offspring. The cat to look for is the one which sires champions. Very often a cat of this type will continue to sire prize-winning kittens over a number of years, even if he is not a champion himself. The reason, as his pedigree will nearly always show, is that he comes from first-class stock and there are champions among his ancestors.

Of course the study and comparison of pedigrees may not be easy for the novice. Why not leave the matter to one of the established breeders? Most of them keep several stud cats, and, from a glance at your own cat's pedigree, will know which would be most suitable. Their names and addresses will be found in the list of Cats at Stud mentioned earlier.

But do not wait until your cat comes in heat before making these arrangements. The services of good stud cats are in demand, and breeders rightly refuse to overwork them. Once the preliminaries are settled it is only necessary to telephone the stud-owner when your queen is ready for mating. This is usually about the second day of the oestrum.

If possible always take your queen to the stud-owner's cattery yourself. However, should you have to send her by railway she will be perfectly safe, and will be met by the stud-owner (or a representative) at the station nearest to his (or her) cattery. Naturally you will notify the stud-owner of the approximate time of your cat's arrival.

Whether your cat travels accompanied or unaccompanied you will want to make sure she has a comfortable journey. A strong draughtproof basket (as described in Chapter 4) is absolutely essential. The inside of the basket should be lined with newspaper and several thicknesses of blanket, while the lower portion of the outside should be covered with strong brown paper secured with string. Label the basket very clearly, using block letters, and in addition to the stud-owner's address, labels should carry your own name and address, just in case anyone needs to get in touch with you. Where possible, telephone-numbers of both parties should also be inserted. Mark the labels TO BE CALLED FOR.

Finally, paste a large label right across the basket bearing the words LIVE CAT – WITH CARE. Also, it is advisable to insure your cat.

Stud fees are payable in advance. Unless you are taking the cat to the stud-owner yourself, it is customary to send the fee, plus return fare, about the same time as you dispatch the cat. Naturally the fee is sent under separate cover.

The stud-owner will advise you when your cat is being returned. If you do not hear for a few days, however, do not be alarmed. Few queens can be mated immediately upon arrival, because they take a little time to settle down in the new surroundings. Also, many stud-owners like to give two matings, perhaps one on the day of the cat's arrival and another the following day. Nevertheless, one service should be sufficient. If the breeder allows another, it is a gesture of goodwill. There is no obligation for him (or her) to do so.

When your cat arrives home she may *not* have left off calling. Therefore be very careful not to let her into the garden for a few days. There is always the possibility that the mating has been unsuccessful, in which case your pet will wander off and find a husband of her own choice.

First signs of pregnancy are a slight swelling of the nipples, and these also become a deeper pink in colour. If after three or four weeks no such signs are noticeable, then possibly the visit to the stud was unsuccessful. Maiden queens are sometimes very difficult in this respect. Most stud-owners, however, will give an additional mating free of charge, but again this is not an obligation.

Let us assume that a family is on the way. The gestation period is from sixty-three to sixty-five days, although many queens vary by a day or so either way. Handle your pet gently during pregnancy, but do not make the mistake of treating her as an invalid. It is perfectly natural for cats to climb and run about, and it would be foolish to restrict them from doing so. Animals have wonderful intuition, and you may be sure your queen knows just how much exercise she needs.

An elaborate diet is not necessary. In fact brood queens should not be allowed to get too fat. Provided your cat is being fed along the lines suggested earlier, no alteration in the diet is necessary for the first five weeks. After that, additional milky food should be given. Do not give milk for at least two hours after a solid meal, however, or tummy upsets may follow. A meal of sardines every few days is better than aperients, or you can give a teaspoon of pure olive oil.

About a fortnight before the kittens are due to arrive you should prepare a bed for them. This can be made from a wooden box about 24 ins wide and 16 ins deep. It should be left partly open in the front. Place it in a secluded corner of the least-occupied room in the house, and raise it slightly off the floor so that it is out of draughts. For lining use plenty of folded newspaper. The queen will tear this up. A small curtain should be strung across the front of the box, which will provide privacy for the queen and also protect the newly-born kittens' eyes.

If possible, your queen should be allowed to discover this bed for herself. By placing her in it you may well find that she sleeps there happily enough previous to the event, but then slinks off and finds a nest of her own choice in which to have the kittens. This will possibly be the airing cupboard or the inside of your wardrobe. She might even decide upon getting into your own bed!

Another point. I have never found a cat that likes to have her kittens in exactly the same spot twice.

Before the kittens are due to arrive, your pet may seem restless or go off her food. She might even walk about miaouing as if wondering what is going to happen to her. On the other hand, she will possibly settle down almost immediately, purring and quite ready to get on with the business.

Some cats love to have their owners near them at these times, others prefer to be left alone. However, it is advisable to remain near at hand, just in case anything should go wrong. It is impossible to say exactly how long the family will take to arrive, because queens vary considerably in this matter. Once the first kitten is born the others usually come in quick succession. Meanwhile you could speak quietly to your pet from time to time. You could also offer a drink of warm milk, but if she rejects it do not worry.

If, after about two hours from the commencement of labour, there is still no sign of the first kitten, it might be advisable to call the vet. This particularly applies if the queen seems exhausted or distressed in any way. Occasionally, for example, a queen will get out of her box and try to expel the kitten while walking round the room.

However, most queens have their kittens without the slightest difficulty, and occasions for anxiety are rare. Usually, after the arrival of the first kitten, the others follow at about half-hourly intervals. This gives the mother time to clean up her babies as they are born. As she licks each kitten the roughness of her tongue puts life into it, and it begins to cry.

Should the kittens arrive in very quick succession, however, it sometimes becomes impossible for the queen to deal with them. This is where you can be helpful. First you should quickly clear away the mucus from each kitten's mouth and nose, then rub it with a rough towel to provide the necessary friction. Next wrap the kittens in a piece of blanket and place them gently in a basket with a well-covered hot-water bottle. As soon as the queen seems ready, place the babies at her side. You will find that she takes over quite happily!

Another minor difficulty which may occur is the severing of the umbilical cord. Each kitten is born in a separate sac. This is split by the queen, who then bites through the cord to free the baby. She then eats the placenta which is expelled after the birth, and which, strange as it may seem, is very good for her. But if your pet is inexperienced, she may not realise what is required of her, and you will have to come to the rescue. Use the finger and thumb of both hands, and so release the kitten from its sac. Then, holding the cord firmly with the finger and thumb of your left hand, use the right hand to break the cord. Do this gently but quickly, and make quite sure that the placenta comes away.

Once the kittens have all arrived, you should remove the soiled bedding and replace with fresh. If the weather is cold, you can slip a well-covered, stone hot water bottle in the bed, then offer your pet a drink of warm milk and glucose. Most queens refuse to leave their kittens for the first day or two, so make sure the sanitary tray is near at hand. Clean drinking-water should also be available.

Do not give your cat meat for a few days after kittening, but let her have all the milky food she cares to take. She can also have steamed or boiled fish. Remember that the rearing of kittens makes heavy demands on a cat, and now is the time to see that she gets extra nourishment. Brand's Beef Essence or Brand's Chicken Essence would help to build her up. Yeast tablets should also be given.

At first the kittens will be so quiet that you do not know they exist. Occasionally, however, a mother cat has difficulty with her milk, and then the babies cry continually. Try massaging the teats with a little olive oil. If the trouble continues, then send for the vet.

Meanwhile you should change the bedding daily. Sprinkle a little insect powder (not DDT) *underneath* the newspaper to keep the kittens free of fleas, and place a small blanket over it.

You will want to know whether the kittens are males or females. A very helpful sex diagram can be obtained from the Cats' Protection League, 29 Church Street, Slough, Bucks SL1 1PW. New fanciers are advised to send for this and study it carefully, because, although the matter sounds easy enough, even experienced breeders make mistakes sometimes. The testicles in a male kitten do not descend until it is several months old, However, by feeling the area slightly lower down, the penis can usually be discovered. With a female it is all much easier, because the tiny vulva is obvious from birth.

Should your queen produce an exceptionally large litter it might be wise to take some of the kittens away from her. The same, of course, applies if she is ill and unable to nurse the kittens herself. You will not wish to part with even one kitten which can be saved, so your solution is a foster-mother. If you do not know of anyone who may be willing to loan you such a cat, then your best plan is to advertise for one. You could try placing a card in the window of your local newsagent. Or a classified advert in a local or national newspaper might bring results. The point is you will have to act quickly if the kittens are to be saved.

Naturally, you must be very careful about the type of cat you admit into your house or cattery. This is not to say that the cat must be a pedigree. An ordinary cat often has a better supply of milk. It is very important, however, that the cat should be healthy, and not suffering from vermin or skin trouble. Inspect it very carefully.

How will you introduce the foster-cat? Unless this is done very carefully she may refuse the orphans. The best way is to wait until she leaves her own family for a meal. Then replace several of her kittens with the same number of pedigree kittens, rubbing the pure-bred kittens against those of the foster-cat so that they all smell alike. You might also rub a little butter on the pedigree babies, so that the foster-mother is encouraged to lick them.

When she returns, watch her reactions carefully. If she settles down to wash the kittens, this usually means that she has accepted them. You can then go away and leave them in her care.

Introduce the remainder of the orphans in the same way. If you do this gradually, the foster-mother will never know that she has been deprived of her own family. Of course, you will have the ordinary kittens humanely put to sleep.

But it is not always possible to find a foster-cat, in which case you may care to try raising the kittens by hand. However, think well about this first, because it is extremely difficult to rear newly-born kittens on artificial food. You will have to feed the kittens at two-hourly intervals, day and night, for at least a week. You must also see that they are kept warm and that the bedding is changed frequently.

You would like to try? Well, the first thing you will need is a special feeding-spoon with a rubber teat attached to it. If possible feed goat's milk. Cow's milk is not nearly concentrated enough for young kittens and they rarely thrive on it. If you cannot get goat's milk, then feed Sherley's Lactol. Warm the food to a temperature of 100 degrees F (38 degrees C), allowing about half a teaspoonful of food for each kitten.

Taking one kitten at a time, smear a very little food on to its lips. Next squeeze a drop of milk on to the tip of the rubber teat and place this to the kitten's mouth. Be careful not to allow too much food in the mouth at once, however, or the kitten may choke while trying to swallow it.

Gradually increase the food as the kittens grow. When they are about a fortnight old they will probably lap from the spoon, which, of course, saves a lot of trouble.

After each meal massage the kittens' tummies. Do this very gently with the fore-finger, using downward strokes. It will help the kittens to digest their food and aid elimination.

Normally, however, the kittens are best left to their mother's care. Try not to handle them more than necessary; and while they are very young try to resist the temptation of showing them to all your friends. A mother-cat rarely objects to an owner encroaching on her privacy but she may well do so from strangers.

Kittens are born blind. Their eyes do not begin to open until they are a week to ten days old, although Siamese kittens often start to open theirs as early as three days old. At first their eyes are very delicate and should not be exposed to the strong light. After a few days, however, you should draw the curtain of the box partly aside and give their eyes an examination. If the lids are at all sticky, gently bathe them with cottonwool dipped into weak Boracic lotion. Then smear on just a touch of vaseline, golden eye ointment or homoeopathic Calendula ointment. If the trouble does not clear up within a day or two it would be wise to consult the vet. This is particularly advisable if there is any discharge or inflammation, because kittens occasionally suffer from a form of conjunctivitis. Usually it can be cured, but expert treatment is essential.

When the kittens are about three weeks old you should begin teaching them to lap. The best way to offer food is from a very shallow saucer. Do not use cow's milk unless it is very creamy. Use goat's milk, Sherley's Lactol, or one of the baby milk foods thickened with a little cereal.

Take one kitten at a time, as described for hand-feeding. Dip your finger in the milk and then smear it round the kitten's mouth. This will whet its appetite, and it will probably start licking the milk off your finger. Now take the saucer and hold it up to the kitten's mouth. It may want to experiment at once, or you may have to persuade it to do so. But do not have more than a teaspoonful of food in the saucer. Remember the size of the kitten. If it tries to take too much food, and this gets up its nose, it will make it splutter. This can be a frightening experience, and it may be some time before the kitten is willing to try again.

For the first few days feed only once a day. After that feed twice daily and then three times. As the kittens grow you should gradually increase the quantity of food. When the kittens are about five or six weeks old, solids can gradually be introduced into the menu. Give a little finely scraped raw meat, or cooked and mashed fish with all the bones removed, or minced and boned rabbit or chicken. But do remember when introducing any new food to do it very gradually, so that you don't upset the kittens' stomachs.

From the time the kittens begin to lap they must be provided with a sanitary tray. Their mother will teach them how to use it. All you need to do is put it down.

At eight or nine weeks old the kittens should be fully weaned and having four small meals a day. Two of these should be solids and the other two of a milky nature as described in Chapter 2. Now you can take the kittens away from their mother during the daytime and return them to her at night. This will encourage the kittens to fend for themselves, and the queen will not miss them so much when they go to new homes. By now you should also be grooming the kittens daily. Not only will this keep them in good condition but it will also help their future owners. If started early enough, kittens never become bad-tempered over the business of grooming; indeed, they look forward to it.

What kind of prices can you ask for the kittens? This will depend upon the breed and the quality of the animals. If you have a kitten which you consider to be especially promising, it might be worth keeping it and selling it at a show after it has won a prize. You could then ask a higher fee. A kitten of exceptionally high standard might even bring an offer from an overseas breeder. British cats are no mean dollar-earners, but of course they do need to be outstanding.

Kittens which you are keeping for show should be injected against Feline Infectious Enteritis, details of which were given in Chapter 3. Show managers take every precaution to eliminate the danger of infection, but where so many animals are collected together under the one roof there is bound to be some risk.

You should also register a prefix with the Governing Council of the Cat Fancy. There is a set fee for this, but the prefix becomes the property of the breeder for life. Fuller particulars can be obtained from the Secretary of the Council, Mrs W. Davis, Dovefields, Petworth Road, Witley, Surrey.

When choosing a prefix try to think of something really original, for it is by the prefix that your cats will become known. Remember that prefixes will not be accepted that bear a close resemblance to any in existence, or to the names of towns, of colours or recognised titles. I know one breeder who chose for her prefix the word 'Cherubino' from Mozart's *Marriage of Figaro*. A singer by profession, she names all her cats after characters from the opera. Another breeder, this time of Siamese cats, decided on the word 'Chionodoxa' for her prefix, the blue Chionodoxa being, of course, the same colour as a Siamese cat's eyes. Other examples include 'Bonavia', the prefix of a well-known breeder of Chinchilla cats; 'Heatherpine', the prefix of a breeder of Abyssinian cats; 'Kyneton', the prefix of a breeder of Burmese cats; and 'Watermill', the prefix of another Siamese breeder.

Meanwhile your queen may have come in heat again – this sometimes happens even while she is nursing kittens. But do not mate her again just yet. Remember she is in low condition. There is a good deal of controversy as to the number of litters a brood queen should be able to rear a year, but most breeders strongly advise spacing the litters as far apart as possible. A maiden queen should not be allowed more than one litter in the first year of her adult life, after which she should be able to rear two litters a year, each consisting of from four to six kittens. Some queens, of course, never produce more than two or three kittens in a litter, and these might be allowed three families a year.

After some experience in breeding and exhibiting you may wish for a stud cat of your own. If you keep several queens, this will save you the necessity of searching for studs for them. It will also mean that you save on stud fees.

Nevertheless, before embarking on stud work, give the matter very careful thought, because it is *not* easy. Never having kept a stud cat myself, I have discussed the matter with several well-known breeders. They all tell me that the work is very interesting but it needs unlimited patience. Also, in addition to a real love of cats, you should have knowledge of how to handle them. You will also require plenty of space.

In Chapter 1 it was pointed out that an adult tom can rarely be kept in the house. Even if you are prepared to risk its unfortunate habit of spraying, the persistent calling for queens can be very disturbing. Again, where there are queens in the house, the animals cannot be allowed to mate indiscriminately.

So an outside stud-house is essential. This must be large enough to be really comfortable, not only for your own cat but for visiting queens. The mature stud cat is unhappy without sufficient work to do, and it is very doubtful whether your own queens will be enough for him.

A good size for the stud-house would be about 9 ft long. It should measure about 7 ft high at the front and 6 ft high at the back, with a depth back to front of 5–6 ft. The house should contain plenty of well-made windows, so that the cat gets as much fresh air and sunshine as possible. It should be absolutely draughtproof.

The stud-house should also contain a separate wire-fronted compartment for visiting queens, so that male and female can get to know each other through the wire partition before mating. This pen can be either a fixture or movable, but it must be large enough to give the queen complete freedom of movement after allowing for her sleeping-box and sanitary tray.

Another essential feature of the stud-house is a wooden shelf for the use of the stud after mating. He jumps on to this shelf to protect himself from the queen, which otherwise might fly at him in her excitement.

Adjoined to the stud-house should be a long, wired-in run, which is absolutely necessary for exercise. Part of the run should consist of grass, but there should also be a good-sized patch of earth for the cat's sanitary arrangements. It is a good idea to plant a tree-trunk in the run. Not only is this useful as a claw-sharpener, but, weather permitting, the cat can stretch out on it and sunbathe.

You have yet to find your stud cat. For your own queens a good out-cross will be necessary, because inbreeding is seldom advised. Your best choice is a young cat of between one and three years old which is already siring good progeny. However, it is unlikely that you will be able to obtain one easily, because experienced studs are rarely offered for sale. If a breeder should have to part with one there is usually a list of would-be purchasers. This especially applies if the cat is siring prize-winners.

Probably you will have to satisfy yourself with a cat of about six months old. In fact this is a good age to buy a future stud, because it should be beginning to reveal its best qualities. The cat you choose should come from sound stock and be of excellent physique. Eye-colour is important, so are a good coat and well-developed limbs. But do not expect to find the ideal cat, because such does not exist. What you want is a healthy animal that shows no outstanding faults.

Disposition is important. Never choose a bad-tempered cat for future stud work, or it might pass on this disagreeable trait to its offspring. Remember that your stud's reputation will depend entirely on the quality of its kittens.

At what age should you put your cat to stud? This usually depends on the breed. Some cats will mate at eight or nine months old if they are allowed to do so. Others, particularly the Long-haired breeds, may not become interested in the opposite sex until about eighteen months old. If your cat is ready, he could be allowed to mate his first queen between ten and twelve months old, but even then he should be used only very sparingly.

Gradually, of course, you can increase the number of matings. Experience will soon show you about how many your stud requires. However, even when a cat is at the height of its virility, few breeders would allow more than three queens a week, for they know the danger of permitting a stud to use up its reserve stamina. The result may be sterility or sickly kittens.

From the time you meet a visiting queen at the railway station, or receive her in your cattery, she is your responsibility. Besides making her as comfortable as possible while she is in your care, you must make sure that she is mated. This is seldom as easy as it may appear, because many queens are nervous and will not mate immediately.

Therefore, never put the female with your stud directly on arrival. If you do so she may get spiteful and injure him. Put her in her own pen and leave her to settle down. After a while you will find that the animals begin to croon to each other, and this is usually a sign that they are ready for mating. Even then a maiden queen might need a little gentle coaxing.

After mating, the stud will jump on to his shelf to get away from the queen. Meanwhile, the queen screams or rolls about. Do not touch either animal at this moment, but wait until the queen begins to wash herself, which she will do with great determination. Now is the time to remove the male. As soon as the queen quietens down you can put her back into her pen or prepare her for the return journey.

One mating should be sufficient, but most breeders like to give two just to make sure. As mentioned earlier, this is a courtesy and not an obligation. But never leave the animals together to mate repeatedly, for this will only exhaust them.

The stud cat must be kept in good condition but not allowed to get fat. During the breeding season, which is approximately from January to August, meals should be increased to three a day. These should consist chiefly of raw meat, but can be varied occasionally with cooked fish or rabbit. A raw egg is strengthening and will be appreciated after mating.

Always make sure that your stud has clean drinking-water handy, because stud work will make him thirsty. Yeast tablets will help to keep him in good condition.

Be sure to examine every visiting queen very thoroughly before penning her. Look carefully at her ears for signs of canker. You should also part the fur, in case of parasites or skin disease. If you think there is the slightest risk of infection, then return the queen immediately – UNMATED. If you are at all doubtful, seek the advice of a vet, but never on any account risk spreading disease to your stud. After the departure of each visiting queen it is advisable to disinfect the stud-house. You should also change the bedding in the queen's pen.

Finally, remember that although your stud cat must live alone, he needs affection. Be sure to visit him every day. Talk to him and pet him. Always see that he has sufficient exercise and that he is well-groomed. In fact, treat him as you do the queens which share your home. When he has no female visitors he can be allowed the companionship of big kittens of, say, four to five months old. Most stud cats can be trusted with kittens of this age, although two males can rarely be allowed to live together after they are about ten months old. For this reason, if you keep more than one stud cat, you should house them separately. You should also make sure that their houses are a good distance apart.

CHAPTER 6

TRAVELLING WITH CATS

FEW CATS make willing travelling companions. Unlike dogs, which eagerly watch their owners preparing for a journey and refuse to be left behind, most cats will do their best to evade you at such times.

There are, of course, exceptions. Practically all Siamese cats make good travellers. So do Manx and some of the other Short-haired breeds. My own Siamese never objected to a railway journey provided he had a lap to sit on, but he would not tolerate buses or cars. Nor did he like to be shut up in his basket.

Personally, I am not in favour of taking a cat about unless compelled to do so. I think they are much happier in their own surroundings. There are times, however, when it is essential to take a cat on a journey – for example, a visit to the vet, a move of house or the annual holiday.

Unless your cat is a well-seasoned traveller never take it about in your arms. If you are crossing a busy thoroughfare the noise and bustle can be very frightening to the stay-at-home type of cat, and it will do its best to escape you. Even if it does not succeed you may get scratched or bitten. A frightened cat is not responsible for its actions.

Every cat or kitten should have its own travelling basket, of which there are several types available. Even if it does not like being shut up, this is the safest method of transport. Of course, there is not the slightest need for your cat to remain in the basket for the whole of the journey. If you are travelling by railway, once you have settled down in the train your pet will probably be far happier on your lap. For the cat which enjoys car travel, the basket might be dispensed with altogether. But put a collar and lead on your cat, so that you are in control of its actions.

Unlike dogs, cats rarely suffer from travel-sickness. But if your pet is very nervous, ask your vet for a tranquillizer for him.

Do not feed anything but lean meat, and this should be given as reasonably long before starting out as possible. The only liquid necessary is water, and again this should be put down well ahead of time. Unless the journey is a very long one, your cat should not need feeding again until you reach your destination. If the journey is of 24 hours or more, then another meal of lean meat can be given. Do resist well-meaning offers from fellow-travellers. Your cat is far better off without a drink of milk or tit-bits. On a very long journey, however, I would not deny it water.

In discussing the problem of travel this might be a good opportunity to mention holiday arrangements. No real animal lover would think of going on holiday and leaving the cat to fend for itself. Centuries of domesticity have made the cat dependent on human beings for food and shelter, and it cannot be expected to revert to the wild state because some thoughtless owner decides to abandon it.

If possible take your cat on holiday with you. For many cat-owners this should not be nearly as difficult as it may appear. Travelling difficulties are easily overcome, and your pet will enjoy the change of air. Do not be afraid of losing it. I have yet to meet a cat which tries to return to its former home *provided it is with its owners*. For several years when I had the use of a seaside bungalow my cat accompanied us on holiday. He enjoyed full freedom, as at home, and we never needed to confine him in any way. Nor did I butter his paws on arrival, although this is a good idea, because the act of licking them clean will occupy your pet's attention and prevent him from wandering.

Of course it may not be so easy to take several cats away with you. Or, if you are staying in a hotel, one cat may not be welcome, and, even if it is, few cats are happy among so many strangers. There is also the possibility that you may be going abroad, in which case your cat would have to go into six months' quarantine on your return. Owing to the risk of rabies, quarantine regulations are very strictly enforced in Britain. This is as it should be, because although cats are not affected by the disease to the same extent as dogs they *are* susceptible to it, and can pass it on to other animals and humans.

Many cat-owners arrange with a neighbour to look after their cats while they are away, and provided the neighbour is reliable, this is an excellent idea. Personally, I feel that much depends on whether the neighbour likes and understands cats. This is not to say that he (or she) needs to fuss continually over them. But kindness is essential. So is an understanding of their requirements.

Often the best solution is a boarding cattery, although care should be taken when choosing one. In Britain, all animal boarding establishments have to be licensed. Even so, some are much better than others. It is therefore advisable to visit the boarding cattery in advance, and, where possible, to inspect the premises your cat will occupy. A personal recommendation is very useful, but, even so, it should be remembered that not all cats are by any means alike. Some will fret badly if separated from their owners for a day, and even go off their food. Others respond to affection immediately. Even the difficult ones, however, will usually settle down, provided they are in the right surroundings.

But do not leave the booking of accommodation for your cat until just before you leave for your own holiday. The good boarding catteries get booked up well in advance. If necessary, the Cats' Protection League or the RSPCA will supply you with names and addresses.

When the time comes to take your cat along, do not forget his inoculation certificate. Few, if any, reputable boarding establishments will accept cats which have not been inoculated against Feline Infectious Enteritis.

If your pet received his inoculation more than a year ago, a booster dose might be advisable. This should be done at least fourteen days before he goes to the cattery, so see your vet as soon as possible.

Do not take too many toys to the cattery because they could easily be mislaid. But it's a good idea to take your cat's sleeping blanket, for this will help him to settle down.

Be surc to acquaint the proprietor of the boarding cattery of any special details regarding your cat's diet. This is not to say you should expect him to provide luxuries, but he will be glad to know whether your cat prefers cooked meat or raw, how often you feed fish, whether the cat likes milk and so on. You should also take the cat's grooming kit.

All that has been said about holiday travel applies to moving house, except that additional precautions are necessary. This is because cats detest upheaval. The sight of furniture being shifted, especially by strange men, can be terrifying to them. The normal course of preparing to decorate a room is enough to send my cat out of the house until all the commotion is over.

If you have no friend with whom you can safely leave your pet, then send it to a local vet or boarding cattery while the removal is under way. When the furniture is installed and you are ready to settle in at the new home, collect the cat and take it there *yourself*. Shut it in a room with its litter tray and all its own possessions, such as sleeping-basket, feeding-dishes and so on. These personal belongings will help the cat to settle down. Later you can persuade the cat to follow you about the house, for no cat is really happy in a new home until it has been on this voyage of exploration. Make sure that the outside doors and all the windows are closed. You can also offer it a meal. However, do not worry if it does not eat much – cats seldom do in strange surroundings.

After several days, you can let your pet into the garden. If you do this just before his meal time, you should have no difficulty in getting him back.

If the worst happens and your cat disappears, then get in

touch with the neighbours near your old address. Ask them to let you know at once if they should see the cat. Also, before moving, it is advisable to leave your new address with the police station, the local tradesmen, the local branch of the RSPCA and any other animal-welfare centre in the neighbourhood.

The cat should wear an elastic collar bearing the new address. If the collar is of a bright colour, it will be noticed more easily.

CHAPTER 7

CAT AND DOG FRIENDSHIPS

FOR MANY families a cat and dog are part of the normal household. Yet there are others who imagine that it is impossible to keep both animals together.

In my experience almost every type of domestic pet will learn to enjoy each other's company provided they are all shown equal affection from their owner. In fact a cat will often become far more attached to a creature of a different species than to its own.

The sight of dog and cat sharing the same basket is not an uncommon one. Even tiny puppies and kittens have been known to show extreme unselfishness towards each other in the all-important business of food.

A friend of mine keeps two dogs, a cat and a blue budgerigar, and on cold days they all snuggle up together by the fire. I also know a Siamese cat and dog which go for country walks together, unaccompanied by their owner. Then there is a Cocker Spaniel which supervises the cat's maternal quarters whenever she has kittens. This dog sits by the bed, and as soon as the happy event takes place, thumps its tail on the floor, as if to announce the safe arrival of the little family.

My own cats and dogs have always been great friends too. Years ago the family cat and dog used to meet my brother and me from school. Do not ask how they knew what time to appear, but they were never late. Nor can I remember one of them ever coming without the other.

Another cat of mine was so attached to an Irish Terrier puppy that she even shared stolen food with it. She would jump on to the table to see if we had carelessly left anything there she fancied. When she was lucky she always threw the choicest tit-bits down to the dog below! Later, when fully grown, this same dog always helped the cat to raise her kittens.

If you are acquiring a new kitten, then have a puppy with it. You will probably find that both animals accept each other from the start. Of course they will play all kinds of wild games together. Possibly the kitten will spit once or twice at the puppy. But do not let that worry you. It is only the feline way of showing that a cat is boss!

Perhaps you already have an adult dog. Then get a cat or kitten. If possible have a kitten, because the dog will mind it less. In fact, as long as you do not make it feel that the kitten has replaced it in your affection, it will probably not mind at all. I know one dog which merely wagged its tail when a new kitten was introduced into the household. After sniffing the newcomer all over, it strolled across to the hearthrug, stretched out and went to sleep. Obviously it had decided that there was little point in altering its way of life for so small a creature.

The introduction of an adult cat and dog may need more careful handling. Whether cat or dog was living with you first, undoubtedly it will be jealous. If the newly-acquired animal is the cat, and it is not used to dogs, it will probably be frightened. Therefore it would be advisable to have the cat's claws trimmed by a vet so that it cannot injure the dog's eyes. It is also a good idea to keep the animals apart for a day or two until they become accustomed to each other's scent. Put the dog in one room and the cat in another, then change them over. Even so, there is bound to be some tension when they meet. If the dog lived with you first, always speak to him and pat him before you handle the cat. Or vice versa. Do not leave the animals together until they have accepted each other's company. When you see them eating from the same dish and sleeping together, you will know that they are friends.

CHAPTER 8

CAT WELFARE

ALL WHO are devoted to cats may find it hard to believe that there are people who do not show these animals kindness. It is difficult to imagine that anyone could excuse himself for ill-treating a cat merely because 'it was all over the house and ate too much food'. Yet, a three-months-old kitten was thrown from the balcony of a block of flats for no other reason.

No animal lover would abandon a female cat because it was going to have kittens; nor would he shut a cat up in an empty house for days without food. It is equally unthinkable that domestic cats could be stolen to sell to research laboratories, or to make into furs. Unfortunately, however, even in Britain, which enjoys a high reputation for the humane treatment of animals, such examples of cruelty occur frequently.

Pain is also inflicted upon animals through ignorance and indifference. There are people who allow cats to breed indiscriminately, knowing that there is very little chance of homes being found for the kittens. There are others who give children a kitten as a plaything and then are callous enough to abandon it if the child loses interest.

The problem of the stray cat is ever-increasing. Every day of the year animal-welfare workers are rescuing and feeding neglected cats and kittens – mother cats which have crept under hedges to have families, ill-treated kittens shivering with fright and miaouing with hunger, litters of newly-born kittens pushed into dustbins and left to starve by brutal owners.

Readers of this book can help to alleviate such suffering

by supporting animal-welfare societies such as the Cats' Protection League, the Royal Society for the Prevention of Cruelty to Animals (RSPCA), Our Dumb Friends' League, the People's Dispensary for Sick Animals (PDSA), the Wood Green Animal Shelter and others.

Merciful work undertaken by these societies includes the detection and reporting of cruelty; first aid for the sick and injured; food for the strays and the hungry; painless death, where absolutely necessary, for the aged and unwanted; and, not least, educational work among children.

First let me tell you something about the work of the Cats' Protection League. This organisation was founded in 1927 and claims to be the only society in the world working exclusively on behalf of cats and kittens.

The League's headquarters are at 29 Church Street, Slough, Bucks, where there is a clinic run as efficiently as any hospital for humans. There are comfortable wards for in-patients and a fully equipped surgery for the treatment of out-patients. There is a reception ward for strays, where they are housed in comfort until claimed by their owners or found good homes, or, in the case of aged and suffering cats, humanely destroyed after all efforts towards rehabilitation have failed.

No cat or kitten ever leaves the League's premises until it has been neutered. The Cats' Protection League strongly advises the neutering of all cats, male and female, other than those used for breeding purposes.

The Cats' Protection League has branches in North London, Birmingham, Coventry, Leicester, Derby, Nottingham, Manchester, Canterbury, Bournemouth, Isle of Wight, Southampton, Truro, Belfast and Dublin as well as in other towns and cities.

Many of these branches run their own clinics with a local veterinary surgeon in attendance. Where there is no clinic, vouchers are provided by the League for people who cannot afford veterinary fees. These people can then take their cats to a veterinary surgeon for free, or part free, treatment.

Other services include loan of travelling baskets, transport facilities, gifts of feline food parcels, free distribution of grass seed (on receipt of a suitably stamped and addressed envelope), temporary accommodation in emergencies (not holiday boarding) and free advice on any matter relating to the cat.

Particulars of membership of The Cats' Protection League can be obtained from the Secretary, Mr A. E. Parratt, Prestbury Lodge, 29 Church Street, Slough, Bucks SL1 1PW. Members receive the League's very informative and interesting magazine *The Cat*, which is in fact the oldest journal devoted entirely to our feline friends.

The work of the RSPCA needs no introduction to animal lovers. It is the oldest and largest of the animal-protection societies, and has been working on behalf of all animals and birds since 1824. In addition to investigating cases of cruelty, the RSPCA runs clinics for the treatment of sick and injured animals, with fully qualified veterinary surgeons in attendance. Its educational work, particularly among children, is resulting everywhere in a more humane treatment of animals. The children attend film shows, listen to talks on animals and attend pet shows, where they have to prove that they know all about the care and feeding of their pets.

So far as cats are concerned, a principal aim of the RSPCA is to prevent the suffering of the cat cast aside to become a stray. This is achieved by extensive publicity in the Press, the distribution of leaflets and so on. For example, just prior to the holiday season, leaflets are widely distributed offering valuable suggestions to cat-owners regarding the welfare of their cats while they themselves are away. These leaflets also remind cat-owners that to leave a cat uncared for is not only callous, but a punishable offence.

In a prosecution brought by the RSPCA, a woman went away from her house on a Monday, leaving her cat. For the next few days the cat's cries were heard, and on the following Saturday an inspector of the RSPCA entered the house to liberate the poor animal. The cat was found to be almost a skeleton. The magistrate inflicted a fine.

The RSPCA encourages kindness by offering medals for animal life-saving. Recently one such medal was awarded to a schoolboy who played a major part in the rescue of a cat from the top of a chimney-stack. Other medals have been awarded to two policemen who discovered, and rescued, eight cats which were tied up in a sack. Fortunately the RSPCA was able to trace the owners of most of these cats.

Perhaps the youngest hero ever to figure in the Society's records is Peter Klonda, aged 3½, who most gallantly saved his brother's Siamese cat, 'Fini', from the jaws of a retriever dog. The children were taking the cat for a walk in the park when the dog attacked 'Fini'. Peter immediately rushed to the rescue and seized 'Fini' in his arms, and although in her frantic terror the cat clawed his face, he did not let her go. The RSPCA presented him with two books, an Animal Defender Badge and a Kindness to Animals Badge.

If you would like details of how you can help the RSPCA, write to the Chief Secretary, The Manor House, Horsham, Sussex RH12.

Many thousands of cats, as well as other animals and birds, owe their lives to the People's Dispensary for Sick Animals (PDSA). Founded in 1917 by the late Mrs Maria Elizabeth Dickin, CBE, it is the only welfare society founded exclusively for the free treatment of sick and injured animals whose owners cannot afford fees.

In addition to treating about a million cases annually in the United Kingdom, the PDSA also carries on its fine work overseas – in France, Morocco, Egypt and South Africa.

Whenever possible the PDSA goes to any animal in distress. By means of its motor caravan dispensaries and ambulances it works in more than 200 towns and villages in Britain, including large industrial areas and remote country hamlets where no other attention is available. Often on a refuse dump or slag heap may be found some injured or half-starved creature which has crept away, as animals will, to endure its sufferings alone.

Here are a few examples of cats which have been brought back to health and happiness by the PDSA:

(*a*) A veterinary officer in charge of a PDSA mobile caravan was stopped in the open countryside by a distracted cat-owner who had spent hours searching for her pet. At last it was found, having caught itself in a bramble hedge, where it had torn a wound in its back on some barbed wire. After being given an anaesthetic to put it temporarily out of its terrible pain, the cat was taken to a PDSA dispensary for treatment. In spite of the severity of its injury it made an excellent recovery.

(*b*) Many unsuccessful attempts had been made to rescue a black cat which had climbed a very high tree and was too frightened to descend. The difficulty was that the branch on which the cat was perched would not support the weight of a ladder and was swaying in the wind. The PDSA ambulance crew solved the problem by sawing the branch off the tree and lowering it with the cat to the ground by ropes.

(*c*) A small male kitten was brought to a PDSA dispensary absolutely devoid of hair. Although it might have seemed that the animal should be put to sleep, the owner was prepared to go to any trouble to avoid this. A long and tedious course of treatment was accordingly embarked upon and was rewarded, for the cat grew a beautiful long white coat and remained in perfect health.

In the general interest, the PDSA will neuter male kittens between the ages of three and six months, but does not undertake the 'doctoring' of females.

Fuller particulars of PDSA activities can be obtained from the Secretary, PDSA House, South Street, Dorking, Surrey.

The Blue Cross (formerly Our Dumb Friends' League) also deserves special mention. Founded in the 1890s, its work is mainly centred on hospitals which provide a complete animal welfare service. Each hospital is equipped with laboratory facilities for speedy tests, X-ray and darkroom, animal quarters and operating theatre. At the Society's central hospital at Victoria, in London, a veterinary surgeon is on call all night, besides the regular night staff. It is also interesting to note that this hospital has never been closed, even through both World Wars, since it was opened in 1906.

The many other animal welfare services run by the Blue Cross include a very modern cats' home outside Cambridge, a first-class modern cattery at Chalfont St Peter in Buckinghamshire, and another at Felixstowe in Suffolk. Cats are also specially catered for at the Blue Cross Home of Rest at Northiam, centred on an old Sussex oast house in six acres of fields.

If you would like to know more about the Blue Cross animal welfare services, write to the Secretary, Animals' Hospital, Hugh Street, Victoria, London SW1V 1QQ.

The welfare of cats and kittens has always played a very big part in the work of the Wood Green Animal Shelter in North London. Here, under the supervision of Dr Margaret Young, neglected, ill-treated, stray and injured animals are given protcction, treatment and care.

Through a special memorial fund for the benefit of cats, arrangements have been made with cat lovers all over Britain who have undertaken to tend sick and ailing cats and help those injured in traps – almost a daily occurrence in country districts.

At the Shelter's country home for stray animals at Heydon, in Hertfordshire, the cats enjoy a natural life, yet cannot get lost or wander away. There are special cat-houses with deep straw beds to sleep on, posts and trees for scratching purposes, bushes to sit under and rafters to climb. There is even a small kitten-house for the youngsters which may not want to mix with staid and older cats!

A similar cat-sanctuary functions at headquarters – a place where lost and homeless cats can be kept under natural conditions until they are claimed by their owners or found good homes.

For fuller particulars write to the Secretary, 601 Lordship Lane, Wood Green, London, N.22.

Mention should also be made of the Mortimer Fund for Cat Welfare, started by the late Adele Rudd and bequeathed to the RSPCA.

Mortimer was a half-Siamese cat of unique appearance, having a white coat with tabby points and tail. He started life as a starving stray, was befriended by Miss Rudd, and soon became the perfect example of what such a cat can look like when given a good home and human companionship.

During his lifetime (he died in 1955) Mortimer was the means of raising large sums of money for animal-welfare societies. He became known as the Ambassador of Strays.

The good work of the Mortimer Fund for Cat Welfare is being continued by the RSPCA, from which full particulars can be obtained.

The Feline Advisory Bureau was founded in 1958 to promote the welfare of all cats, to raise the status of the cat, and to raise the standard of veterinary knowledge and treatment. Services include:

1. The advice of highly qualified experts on special problems of health, feeding, general care and genetics to improve feline health standards.
2. Lists of recommended boarding catteries.
3. Lists of veterinary surgeons specialising in small animal practice including those who are able to attend cats at night.
4. Advice on acquiring kittens and studs to assure healthy cats.
5. Advice on cattery construction.
6. Advice on show preparation.

The Bureau runs a very interesting quarterly bulletin which all members receive. It also organises meetings, discussion groups, lectures and film shows on cat welfare. For fuller particulars, write to the Hon. Secretary, Michael A. Findlay, BVMS, MRCVS, 6 Woodthorpe Road, Putney, London SW15 6UQ.

CHAPTER 9

LONG-HAIRED CATS

All your wondrous wealth of hair,
Dark and fair,
Silken-shaggy, soft and bright
As the clouds and beams of night,
Pays my reverent hand's caress
Back in friendlier gentleness.

—SWINBURNE

THE BEAUTY of a Long-haired cat is difficult to surpass. Dignity comes natural to it. Whether pedigree or otherwise, the Persian cat, as it is usually called, makes an affectionate and gentle pet. Provided it is kept in good condition it also makes a fine show cat.

It is sometimes thought that the Persian cat is less intelligent than the Short-hair. This is not necessarily so. Solemn by nature, it may be slightly less temperamental. Otherwise, it is playful, plaintive, dozy or demonstrative, like any other cat. Some of them show amazing intelligence, and I have yet to meet one which is dull.

At one time Long-haired cats were known as French cats because they came from Paris. Most of them were pure white with beautiful, long, silky hair. Their owners were very fond of decorating them with huge ornamental bows of ribbon. Harrison Weir, the famous nineteenth-century writer on cats, described them as 'the valued, pampered pets of West End Life'.

Later, coloured Long-haired cats were imported into Britain. There was the Angora Cat, the Persian Cat, the

Russian Cat and the Indian Cat. There was also a variety known as the Carthusian Friar. It was a blue cat with very long, silky fur.

But the Angora and the Persian were definitely the most popular. Not that there was so very much difference between them. Both cats had long coats, but while the Angora's was of woolly texture, the Persian's was silky. The other chief difference appears to have been in the matter of features. The Angora had a pointed face, while that of the Persian was rounder. Both cats had large and very expressive eyes.

Angora cats were said to be great favourites of the Turks and Armenians. They particularly prized the white variety with blue eyes, although colours included almost every tint imaginable. You could have had your cat in slate-blue, fawn, deep red, mottled grey or, in fact, any shade to tone in with the Eastern furniture.

Black appears to have been the most popular colour in Persians. Harrison Weir tells us (*Our Cats and All About Them*, 1889): 'A good rich, deep black, with orange-coloured eyes and long flowing hair, grand in mane, large and with graceful carriage, with a mild expression, is a truly and very beautiful object, and one very rare'. He describes one such cat called Mimie, which followed its master about like a dog and always sat on the table by his side while he wrote letters or attended to business matters. This cat was a consistent prize-winner and wore a handsome collar upon which were inscribed her many victories. The collar and all her food were earned by the cat herself and paid for out of prize-money.

Nowadays the Blue Persian is easily the most popular of the Long-haired breeds of cat recognised by the Governing Council of the Cat Fancy. This lovely breed was first shown to the public at the Crystal Palace in the early 1880s, by Miss Frances Simpson, a leading cat-breeder of those days. Some kittens were exhibited in a class of mixed colours. They caused a great sensation.

By 1889 Blue Persians had become so popular that special

classes were introduced for them at the shows. Some twelve years later Frances Simpson founded the Blue Persian Cat Society, which has flourished ever since. If you want to see what a good Blue Persian really looks like, go to this Society's annual show, held usually in autumn. Particulars of venue will be found in the Cat periodicals.

The real beauty of a Blue Persian lies in its long, silky coat and brilliant copper eyes. Any shade of blue is allowable, from dark blue to the palest lavender, but the lighter colours are definitely the most sought after. Evenness of colour is very important. When the hairs are parted they should be completely free from markings or any change of tint right down to the roots.

A Blue Persian has a broad, rounded head, with well-developed cheeks and short, tip-tilted nose. The ears of a good specimen are tiny and well-tufted. There should be great width between them. The eyes are large and full, and very expressive.

One of the most attractive features of the Blue Persian is the massive, well-groomed frill, which extends well over its shoulders. The body is very cobby, which means that it is low-set but not coarse or angular. The tail is short and full. The following is the official standard of points for the Blue Long-hair:

Coat Any shade of blue allowable, sound and even in colour; free from markings, shadings or any white hairs. Fur long, thick and soft in texture. Frill full.

Head Broad and round, with width between the ears. Face and nose short. Ears small and tufted. Cheeks well developed.

Eyes Deep orange or copper; large, round and full, without a trace of green.

Body Cobby, and low on the legs.

Tail Short and full, not tapering (a kink shall be considered a defect).

Members should not be deterred from showing their cats if they do not come up to the high standard set forth in the above definition.

SCALE OF POINTS

Coat	20
Condition	10
Head	25
Eyes	20
Body	15
Tail	10
Total	100

CREAM LONG-HAIR

The Cream Persian is another very popular Long-haired breed. As with the Blue, its coat is the chief attraction. In a good specimen this is a pale, rich cream, almost like Devonshire cream in appearance. Again it is important that the colour of the fur should be the same all over the body, from the tip of each hair right down to the roots. There must be no white markings on the cat's undercoat or tail. Nor should there be any tabby bars anywhere.

Cream Persians first appeared towards the end of the nineteenth century. Their origin, however, is something of a mystery. One of the earliest specimens was a cat called 'Ripon', said to have been produced from the mating of a Blue Persian and an Orange Persian. In those days Cream Persians were also known as 'Fawn Persians', owing to a reddish tint in the coat, chiefly the result of breeding them from Red cats and from Tortoiseshells. This 'hot cream colour', as modern judges term it, may still persist when Creams are mated to Creams over a very long period. To eradicate the fault, experienced breeders advise mating Cream Persians with Blue Persians. For example, if your queen is too dark in colour, then mate her to a very pale Blue stud. If possible try to find one with two or three Blacks in the pedigree. Strange as it may seem, the black clears the cream colour, and the kittens are usually of a beautiful pale cream.

Standard of Points for Cream Long-hairs

Colour To be pure and sound throughout without shading or markings.
Coat Long, dense and silky, tail short and flowing.
Body Cobby and solid, short thick legs.
Head Broad and round, small ears well set and well tufted, short broad nose, full round cheeks.
Eyes Large and round, deep copper colour.

SCALE OF POINTS

Colour, pale to medium	30
Coat and condition	20
Body	15
Head	20
Eyes	15
Total	100

WHITE LONG-HAIR

With its long, flowing coat, soft and silky in texture, the White Persian is a beautiful creature. But, of course, the coat must be pure white. There must be no markings or shadings of any kind, nor should there be any tinge of yellow. Careful and constant grooming is required. If you live in a town, perhaps a Black Persian would be the wiser choice!

There are three recognised breeds of White Long-hair – the Blue-eyed White, the Orange-eyed White and the Odd-eyed White. The Odd-eyed White should have one deep-blue eye and one orange eye. It makes a very useful cat for breeding.

The green-eyed White Persian is not a recognised variety, and can only be shown in the household pet classes. The same applies to white cats which have one blue eye and one green eye. Nevertheless, they all make delightful pets, being extremely intelligent and gentle with children.

Perhaps you have heard that all white cats are deaf? This is not necessarily so, although, unfortunately, it does apply to many Blue-eyed White cats. Fanciers have done much to breed out this affliction. The trouble is that sound-hearing white cats do not necessarily produce sound-hearing white kittens. Even after two or three years of breeding cats with normal hearing, a whole litter of deaf kittens may appear.

Of course, everyone prefers a cat of sound hearing. But, as with human afflictions, there is usually some form of compensation, and it is comforting to know that deafness rarely, if ever, prevents a cat from enjoying a normal life. In fact, many white cats are so sensitive to vibrations that it is sometimes difficult to realise that they *are* deaf. A friend of mine keeps several cats, including a deaf white one. She talks to them all, and gets exactly the same type of response from them all, including the white one. Even stranger is the fact that when she returns from an outing it is the white cat which is at the door to greet her!

Orange-eyed Whites are not deaf. What is more, they are much easier to breed than the blue-eyed variety. Mate your White Persian queen to a pale Blue Persian stud with deep copper eyes and you should get some lovely kittens. If you want Blue-eyed Whites, however, then you must prepare to be patient. Breeders tell me that even by mating a blue-eyed female to a blue-eyed stud it is impossible to know if the kittens will have blue eyes. Some breeders suggest an outcross, others find that this makes little difference.

However, this is where an odd-eyed cat may be useful. If you can find an odd-eyed queen of blue-eyed parents and mate it to an odd-eyed stud, also of blue-eyed parentage, you should get good results. Such a mating should produce orange-eyed kittens and blue-eyed kittens. The blue-eyed kittens usually have very deep blue eyes.

Standard of Points for Blue-eyed White Long-hairs

Colour Pure white, without mark or shade of any kind.

Coat Long and flowing on body, full frill and brush, which should be short and broad; the coat should be close and soft and silky, not woolly in texture.

Body Cobby and massive, without being coarse, with plenty of bone and substance, and low on the leg.

Head Round and broad, with plenty of space between the ears, which should be small, neat and well covered, short nose, full cheeks and broad muzzle.

Eyes Large, round and wide open, deep blue in colour.

Orange-eyed Whites

Points as above, except for eye-colour, which should be orange or copper.

Note. Whites are very liable to get yellow stains on their tails from accumulated dust, etc. This very damaging peculiarity should be carefully attended to and stains removed before showing.

SCALE OF POINTS

Colour	25
Coat	20
Body	20
Head	20
Eyes	15
Total	100

Black Long-hair

What is more striking than a coal-black Persian cat with brilliant orange eyes? Unfortunately, however, there are not many to be seen in Britain, not even at the cat-shows. The fact is that a Black Long-hair which is really true to type is extremely difficult to produce. In shape and size it resembles any typical Persian, but the coat must be raven black to the roots. This means that there are no white hairs or patches of reddish-brown anywhere. Kittens born with rusty-coloured coats often develop beautiful jet-black fur after they are about six months old. Even so, the coat is easily spoilt by exposure to rain or strong sunlight.

You may imagine that the best Black Persians are obtained from self-coloured matings, but this is seldom so. Here is another example where cross-mating with Blues is often valuable. The pedigree of almost any good Black will show Blues among its ancestors. The late Cyril Yeates, one-time Chairman of the Governing Council of the Cat Fancy, and a great authority on this breed, recommended the crossing of Blacks with Orange-eyed Whites. He claimed that such matings would produce pure white or pure black kittens, and the colour of the Black ones would be absolutely sound to the roots. There are other breeders who have been successful by mating Blacks to Brown Tabbies, Red Tabbies, Tortoiseshells or Creams.

Of course Black cats have always been surrounded by superstition. If a Black Persian cat walks across a bride's path as she is leaving the church after her wedding ceremony, this is said to be a sign of good luck. Should the cat sneeze, the couple will be happy throughout their married life.

Theatrical folk have great faith in Black cats, especially if these happen to have odd eyes. Ellen Terry kept dozens of cats, including black ones, and we are told that she never tired of playing with them or admiring their graceful movements. Peg Woffington, the famous actress of Drury Lane, is said to have been given her first chance by taking a Black Persian to the manager, who was devoted to these creatures.

Standard of Points for Black Long-hairs

Colour	Lustrous raven black to the roots, and free from rustiness, shading, white hairs or markings of any kind.
Coat	Long and flowing on body, full frill and brush, which should be short and broad.
Body	Cobby and massive, without being coarse, with plenty of bone and substance, and low on the leg.
Head	Round and broad, with plenty of space between the ears, which should be small, neat and well covered, short nose, full cheeks and broad muzzle.
Eyes	Large, round and wide open, copper or deep orange in colour, with no green rim.

Note. Black Long-haired kittens are often a very bad colour up to five or six months, their coats being grey or rusty in parts, and sometimes freely speckled with white hairs. Fanciers should not condemn them on this account if good in other respects, as these kittens frequently turn into the densest Blacks.

SCALE OF POINTS

Colour	25
Coat	20
Body	20
Head	20
Eyes	15
Total	100

CHINCHILLA

The Chinchilla is a silvery-coated cat with emerald eyes. To many fanciers it is the most beautiful of the Long-haired breeds, and there are even those who claim that it is the most beautiful of all cats

Looking at a Chinchilla from a distance you might easily mistake it for a white cat. The undercoat *is* white, but the fur on the back, flanks, head, ears and tail is tipped with black. In a good specimen this tipping is so evenly distributed that it gives the appearance of sparkling silver. Another very attractive feature of the Chinchilla is a brick-red nose.

The story of the first Chinchilla goes back to a chance mating of a Blue Persian with a stray tom. In the resultant litter was a smoke-coloured kitten which was given the name of Chinnie. Later this cat was mated to a Silver Tabby, and one of the females from their progeny produced the first Chinchilla male. The cat was called 'Silver Lambkin'. It became very famous, and lived for seventeen years.

In addition to its fascinating appearance the Chinchilla has a very affectionate nature. Contrary to some beliefs, it is also a very hardy breed. One of Britain's foremost breeders of Chinchillas keeps all her cats outside, and in all weathers. 'The older they grow the more beautiful they become,' she once told me. Proof of this was, of course, when 'Champion Langherne Winsome', a lovely Chinchilla female, was judged 'Best Cat in Show' at 12½ years old.

Several breeders are now producing Blue Chinchillas. These are very beautiful, their coats being tipped with blue rather than black.

Standard of Points for Chinchillas

Colour The undercoat should be pure white, the coat on the back, flanks, head, ears and tail being tipped with black, this tipping to be evenly distributed, thus giving the characteristic sparkling silver appearance; the legs may be very slightly shaded with the tipping, but the chin, ear tufts, stomach and chest must be pure white; any tabby markings or brown or cream tinge is a defect. The tip of the nose should be brick-red, and the visible skin on the eyelids and the pads should be black or dark brown.

Head	Broad and round, with breadth between ears which should be small and well-tufted; wide at the muzzle; snub nose.
Shape	Cobby body; short, thick legs.
Eyes	Large, round and most expressive, emerald or blue-green in colour.
Coat and Condition	Silky and fine in texture, long and dense, extra long on frill.
Tail	Short and bushy.

SCALE OF POINTS

Colour	25
Head	20
Shape	15
Eyes	15
Coat and Condition	15
Tail	10
Total	100

Tortoiseshell Long-hair

'I have a kitten, my dear, the drollest of all creatures that wore a cat's skin. She is dressed in a tortoiseshell suit....'

Thus wrote William Cowper to Lady Hesketh in 1787.

The Tortoiseshell is a patched cat. The three colours –

which are black, red and cream – should be bright and rich. They also need to be well broken, so that they blend into each other and give the required 'patched' appearance. The coat is patched, the face is also patched, as are the short, thick legs and bushy tail. Eyes are deep orange or copper.

Not only is a Tortie a most attractive cat in itself, but, if mated wisely, a good queen will usually produce a lovely assortment of kittens. Tortoiseshell males are very rare indeed, and when one does appear it is almost always sterile. To date there have been only three recorded examples of virile Tortie males. One of these lived in Devon and made cat history by siring sixty-five kittens in two years.

An amusing story tells how, during the nineteenth century, a Tortoiseshell male was secured at an auction for £22. The proud owner brought the cat home and decided to bath it. The colours may have been bright but, unfortunately, they were not fast. Puss emerged from his bath a very charming, but quite ordinary, black-and-white cat!

To breed from a Tortoiseshell, then, cross-mating will be necessary. A good plan is to use a male of one of the self-colours in the queen's coat. If you can find one which was bred from a Tortoiseshell dam, so much the better. From such a mating you could expect to get self-coloured red, black or cream kittens. If you are very lucky you might even get a Tortoiseshell kitten.

Another way is to mate your Tortie to a Blue stud. Many breeders prefer this method, because, in addition to the colours already mentioned, there is the possibility of Blue Long-haired kittens and also of Blue-Creams. Such a mating should also help to fix 'type' in the progeny.

Standard of Points for Tortoiseshell Long-hairs

Colour Three colours, black, red and cream, well broken into patches; colours to be bright and rich and well broken on the face.

Coat Long and flowing, extra long on frill and brush.
Body Cobby and massive, short legs.
Head Round and broad, ears small, well-placed and well-tufted; short broad nose, full round cheeks.
Eyes Large and round, deep orange or copper.

SCALE OF POINTS

Coat	50
Body	15
Head	20
Eyes	15
Total	100

Tortoiseshell-and-White Long-hair

As the name implies, this breed differs from the Tortoiseshell only by the addition of white patches. Again, most of these cats are females.

The Tortoiseshell-and-White cat is more common than the Tortoiseshell, but it is rare to find a really good one. As with most cats with white markings, there is all too often a tendency for these to appear where they are least wanted. Nevertheless, if your cat is to become a prize-winner the four colours must be clear and well defined. It is desirable, for example, that the Tortoiseshell-and-White cat should have a really good patch of white on the chest. The legs and feet should be pure white and there should be a blaze of white running up the face. There must be no stray white hairs in the coloured patches and no tabby markings anywhere.

Standard of Points for Tortoiseshell-and-White Long-hairs

Colour The three colours, black, red and cream, to be well distributed and broken and interspersed with white.
Coat Long and flowing, extra long on brush and frill.

Body	Cobby and massive, short legs.
Head	Round and broad; ears small, well-placed and tufted; short broad nose, full round cheeks.
Eyes	Large and round, deep orange or copper.

SCALE OF POINTS

Coat	50
Body	15
Head	20
Eyes	15
Total	100

Blue-Cream Long-hair

As the name suggests, this beautiful variety has a coat of blue and cream. In the United States it is known as the Blue Tortoiseshell. But this is not an entirely accurate description because the Tortie wears a coat of three colours, whereas that of the Blue-Cream consists only of two. Moreover, the Tortoiseshell's colours are distributed in solid patches, while those of the Blue-Cream, according to the British show standard, should be 'softly intermingled'. When this occurs it gives the cat a hazy, shot-silk effect which is really beautiful. The best specimens have a soft, profuse coat and coppery-red eyes.

Fertile Blue-Creams are always females, and in this respect they do resemble Tortoiseshells. Also, like the Tortie, they are very interesting cats for the breeder. This is because it is possible to get Blue, Cream and Blue-Cream kittens in the same litter or at different times.

Standard of Points for Blue-Cream Long-hairs

Colour and Markings	To consist of blue and cream, softly intermingled, pastel shades.
Coat	To be dense and very soft and silky.

Head	Head broad and round, tiny ears, well-placed and well-tufted, short broad nose, colour intermingled on face.
Eyes	Deep copper or orange.
Body	Short, cobby and massive; short, thick legs.

SCALE OF POINTS

Colour	30
Coat and Condition	20
Head	20
Eyes	15
Body	15
Total	100

SMOKE

The Smoke Persian is a cat of contrasts. Its long, silky fur is black on the top and shades to silvery-white at the roots. Thus the cat's back appears to be dense black, while the sides and flanks are silver. The head and face are jet black. The ears are black with silver tips. The frill is silver. The paws are jet black.

Mention should also be made of the Blue Smoke, a beautiful but very rare variety. Here the fur is dark blue, shading to a much paler colour at the roots. Therefore the cat has a dark-blue face and head which are set off by a very pale-blue ruff. The back is dark blue, shading to paler blue on the sides and flanks. The ears are very dark blue, but the ear-tufts are pale blue, in fact almost white. The paws are dark blue.

Most Smoke kittens are born very dark and some months may pass before the colour contrast becomes apparent.

Standard of Points for Smokes

A Smoke is a cat of contrasts, the undercolour being as ash-white as possible, with the tips shading to black, the dark points being most defined on the back, head and feet, and the light points on frill, flanks and ear-tufts.

Colour	Body: Black, shading to silver on sides, flanks and mask. Feet: Black with no markings. Frill and ear-tufts: Silver. Undercolour: As nearly white as possible.
Coat and Condition	Silky in texture, long and dense, extra long frill.
Shape	Head: Broad and round, with width between ears, which should be small and tufted; snub nose. Body: Cobby, not coarse but massive, short legs.
Eyes	Orange or copper in colour, large and round in shape, pleasing expression.
Brush	Short and bushy.

SCALE OF POINTS

Colour: Body, mask and feet, frill and ear-tufts and undercolour	40
Coat texture and condition	10
Head (including ears)	20
Body	15
Eyes	10
Brush	5
Total	100

Note. The above is also the standard for Blue Smokes, except that where the word 'black' occurs, 'blue' should be substituted.

Red Self Long-hair

This is a very beautiful cat – the real Red Persian. It is also an extremely rare cat. The colour must be a deep, warm red, and there must be no tabby bars or markings.

To breed the Red Persian would present a challenge. Some breeders suggest using a very lightly marked Red Tabby queen and mating it with a deep Cream Persian stud. Others prefer to use a Tortoiseshell queen and mate her to a Black stud. A well-known American breeder once told me that she had tried the above crosses as well as many others. Eventually she came to the conclusion that the darkest and most 'typy' red kittens were produced only by using Red cats. In other words, the darkest and most solid reds come from colour-bred cats, not from using an out-cross.

Standard of Points for Red Self Long-hairs

Colour Deep rich red, without markings.
Coat Long, dense and silky, tail short and flowing.
Body Cobby and solid, short thick legs.
Head Broad and round, small ears well set and well tufted, short broad nose, full round cheeks.
Eyes Large and round, deep copper colour.

SCALE OF POINTS

Coat	50
Body	15
Head	20
Eyes	15
Total	100

Red Tabby Long-hair

The Red Tabby Persian is much better known than the Red Self, and is full of personality. Its ground colour should be red, and it should have clearly and boldly defined deep

BRITISH BLUE KITTEN

BURMESE KITTENS

CHINCHILLA

CREAM PERSIAN AND KITTENS

SILVER TABBY LONG-HAIR

ABYSSINIANS

DOG AND CAT FRIENDSHIP

WHITE SHORT-HAIR

WHITE PERSIAN

WHITE MANX

PERSIAN KITTENS

BLACK PERSIAN

BLUE PERSIAN

SEAL-POINTED SIAMESE

red markings on the head and face, along the back, down the chest and on the legs and tail. If you wish to breed from a Red Tabby never buy one with white markings, for these are very difficult to eradicate. If, however, you just want a household pet, such markings need not bother you.

Standard of Points for Red Tabby Long-hairs

Colour and Markings	Deep, rich, red colour, markings to be clearly and boldly defined, continuing on down the chest, legs and tail.
Coat	Long, dense and silky, tail short and flowing; no white tip.
Body	Cobby and solid, short thick legs.
Head	Broad and round, small ears, well set and well tufted, short broad nose, full round cheeks.
Eyes	Large and round, deep copper colour.

SCALE OF POINTS

Coat	50
Body	15
Head	20
Eyes	15
Total	100

Brown Tabby Long-hair

This is another lovely variety, full of character and intelligence. The coat is a rich, tawny sable with dense black markings.

A well-known breeder of Brown Tabbies has described these cats as 'real tigers in the home'. In fact, there was a time when all striped cats were known as Tiger cats. The word Tabby was derived from 'Atabi silk', a kind of taffeta, which was first imported into Britain from Baghdad. One day a prospective buyer was looking over this material and likened the water-marks on it to the bars and horseshoes on his cat's coat. From that day onwards the Tiger cat became the Tabby.

Standard of Points for Brown Tabby Long-hairs

Colour and Markings	Rich tawny sable, with delicate black pencillings running down face. The cheeks crossed with two or three distinct swirls. The chest crossed by two unbroken narrow lines, butterfly markings on the shoulders. Front of legs striped regularly from toes upwards. The saddle and sides to have deep bands running down them, and the tail to be regularly ringed.
Coat	Long and flowing, tail short and full.
Body	Cobby and massive, short legs.
Head	Round and broad, small well-placed and well-tufted ears, short broad nose, full round cheeks.
Eyes	Large and round, hazel or copper colour.

SCALE OF POINTS

Coat	50
Body	15
Head	20
Eyes	15
Total	100

SILVER TABBY LONG-HAIR

For many cat lovers this is the most attractive of the Tabby breeds. A good specimen is certainly a beautiful animal. The coat is a lovely pale silver and the pencillings are jet black. Unfortunately, however, there are very few really well-marked Silver Tabby Long-hairs to be seen. The reason is that the longer the coat the more blurred the markings become. Naturally this is a disadvantage in the show-pen.

Several breeders suggest that crossing with a Silver Tabby Short-hair improves both the colour and the markings of the Long-haired Silver Tabby. Other possible outcrosses are the Black Long-hair or the Chinchilla. The latter has the advantage of possessing the desired green eyes.

Standard of Points for Silver Tabby Long-hairs

Colour	Ground colour pure pale silver, with decided jet black markings, any brown tinge a drawback.
Head	Broad and round, with breadth between ears and wide at muzzle, short nose, small well-tufted ears.
Shape	Cobby body, short thick legs.
Eyes	Colour: Green or hazel.
Coat and Condition	Silky in texture, long and dense, extra long on frill.
Tail	Short and bushy.

SCALE OF POINTS

Colour	40
Head	20
Shape	10
Coat and Condition	15
Tail	5
Eyes	10
Total	100

COLOURPOINT LONG-HAIR

Colourpoints, or Himalayans as they are known in the USA, are among the most popular of the Long-haired breeds.

This is not surprising because they are very beautiful, having the colour and markings of the Siamese cat, but the structure and long, flowing coat of the Persian.

They are very friendly and affectionate, and very hardy. But they are *not* Long-haired Siamese cats, as some people wrongly imagine. They only resemble the Siamese in coat pattern.

Standard of Points for Colourpoint Long-hairs

Coat Fur long, thick and soft in texture, frill full.

Colour (i) Seal points with cream body colour. (ii) Blue points with glacial white body colour. (iii) Chocolate points with ivory body colour. (iv) Lilac points with magnolia body colour. (v) Red points with off-white body colour. (vi) Tortie points with cream body colour. Points to be of solid colour, and body shading, if any, to tone with the points.

Head Broad and round with width between the ears. Face and nose short. Ears small and tufted and cheeks well developed.

Eyes Shape: large, round and full. Colour: clear, bright and decidedly blue.

Body Cobby and low on leg.

Tail Short and full, not tapering. A kink shall be considered a defect.

Note. Any similarity in TYPE to Siamese to be considered undesirable and incorrect.

SCALE OF POINTS

Coat	15
Points and Body-colour	10
Head	30
Shape of eye	10
Colour of eye	10
Body	15
Tail	10
Total	100

BI-COLOURED LONG-HAIR

Standard of Points for Bi-coloured Long-hairs

Colours and Distribution	Any solid colour and white, the patches of colour to be clear, even and well distributed. Not more than two thirds of the cat's coat to be coloured and not more than a half to be white. Face to be patched with colour and white.
Coat	Silky texture. Long and flowing, extra long on frill and tail.
Head	Round and broad with width between the ears, which should be small, well placed and tufted. Short broad nose, full cheeks, wide muzzle and firm chin (level bite).
Body and Legs	Body cobby and massive, short thick legs.
Eyes	Large and round, set well apart, deep orange or copper in colour.
Tail	Short and full.
Serious Faults	Tabby markings; a long tail; yellow or green eyes.

SCALE OF POINTS

Colour	25
Coat	15
Body	15
Tail	5
Head	25
Eyes	15
Total	100

Birman

The Birman was first imported into Britain in 1965 by Mrs Elsie Fisher of London, after she had seen this lovely breed in Paris. Claimed to be descended from the sacred cats which were kept in the temples of the East, it has a very spectacular appearance as well as a gentle and affectionate nature. Its coat is long and thick, with a dense ruff and bushy tail. It has the colouring of a Siamese, except that its feet and the backs of its hind legs are snow white.

Since importing her first Birmans, Mrs Fisher has bred 36 Champions, International Champions and Grand Champions, and has exported them to many countries of the world.

Standard of Points for Birmans

Body	Long but low on the legs. Short, strong paws. Four white paws; the white on the two back paws has to go up the back of the legs to a point, like a gauntlet.
Head	Wide, round and strongly built, with full cheeks.
Fur	Long with good, full ruff, bushy tail, silky texture, slightly curled on belly.
Eyes	Bright China blue.
Tail	Bushy (not short).
Colour and Condition	The colouring is the same as Siamese, Seal and Blue but face (mask), tail and paws are dark brown with the Seals, and blue/grey with the Blues. However, the beige of the coat is slightly golden. The paws are white gloved, this being the characteristic of the Birman cat.

SCALE OF POINTS

Body	20
Head	20
Fur	25
Eyes	5
Tail	10
Colour and Condition	20
Total	100

Turkish Cats

This is another very interesting cat. It has a long, white, silky coat with auburn markings on the head and a most attractive auburn-ringed tail. Its eyes are large and round, pink-rimmed and pale amber in colour. The tip of its nose is shell-pink, as are the insides of its ears and the footpads.

But perhaps the most remarkable thing about the Turkish cat is that it has absolutely no fear of water. Unlike most cats, it enjoys being bathed, although the water must be heated to 101 degrees F (about 38 degrees C) and the cat must be thoroughly dried afterwards.

Turkish cats are also groomed differently from other Long-haired breeds. Having no thick woolly undercoat, they should never be brushed and only combed occasionally.

Standard of Points for Turkish Cats

Colour and Coat	The coat should be chalk white with no trace of yellow. Auburn markings on face with white blaze. Ears should be white; nose tip, pads and inside ears should be a delicate shell pink. Fur should be long, soft and silky to the roots. No woolly undercoat.
Head	Short wedge and well-feathered, large ears, upright and set fairly close together; long nose.

Eyes	Shape should be round, colour should be light amber, rims should be pink-skinned.
Body	Long but sturdy, legs medium in length, neat, round feet with well-tufted toes. Males should be particularly muscular on neck and shoulders.
Brush	Full, medium length, auburn in colour with faint auburn rings in cats, more distinct ring markings in kittens.

Note. This is the ideal. Occasionally some cats may have small auburn markings irregularly placed but this should not disqualify an otherwise good specimen.

SCALE OF POINTS

Coat and colour	35
Head	25
Eyes	10
Body	10
Brush	10
Condition	10
Total	100

Chocolate and Lilac Long-hairs

Both of these new varieties are cats of striking beauty. As their names imply, one is chocolate colour all over and the other is pale lilac. Both have orange eyes.

Owners of these Self-Chocolate and Self-Lilac cats declare that they make delightful pets. In addition to their ornamental appearance, they are very gentle and affectionate. Furthermore, they need less grooming than many of the other Long-haired breeds.

Cameo Persians

At present the Cameo Persians are better known in the USA than in Britain. Nevertheless, they are to be seen occasionally at the larger cat shows.

There are four varieties – Shell, Shaded, Smoke and Tabby.

The Shell Cameo has a pure white undercoat, the fur on its back, flanks, head and tail being delicately tipped with red. This gives a lovely sparkling appearance. The face and legs are lightly shaded with red, while the ear-tufts, chest, chin and tummy are white. The eyes are copper or orange.

The Shaded Cameo is much darker than the Shell, and the Smoke Cameo is darker still. The Tabby Cameo has a cream coat with deep red tabby markings.

Balinese

These are pure-bred Siamese cats with long hair. No cross mating with other breeds has ever taken place to produce the length of coat. Also, they have all the Siamese characteristics.

At the time of writing, the first ever litter of Balinese kittens has just been bred in Britain. They are from two cats imported from the USA.

CHAPTER 10

BRITISH SHORT-HAIRED CATS

When the tea is brought at five o'clock
And all the neat curtains are drawn with care,
The little black cat with bright green eyes
Is suddenly purring there.

—HAROLD MONRO

NO ANIMAL makes a more charming companion than a glossy, Short-haired cat. As a vermin-killer you will not find a better worker. Domesticated by the Egyptians, the Short-haired cat is undoubtedly the best known of all cats. It is to be seen on farms, in shops and offices, as well as sitting outside garden gates or curled up on the hearthrug of millions of British homes.

There are numerous varieties of Short-haired cats, including Ginger cats, Sandy cats, Marmalade cats, Black cats, Black-and-White cats, White-and-Black cats and Tabbies of all descriptions. Then, of course, there are the Pedigree Short-haired cats. These fall into two groups: British Short-hairs and Foreign Short-hairs. Last, but far from least, there is that fascinating creature, the tailless Manx.

Almost all the Long-haired breeds which were described in Chapter 9 have their Short-haired counterparts. These are known as the British Pedigree Short-hairs. With the exception of the Manx, which is also regarded as British, they should all conform to the same type. This means that the head is broad between the ears, which are small and slightly rounded at the tips. The face and nose are short, but not so short as those of a Persian cat. The cheeks are well developed. Eyes are large and round.

A Short-haired cat should have a well-knit and powerful

body, a full and broad chest, and a tail which is thick at the base, but should be short rather than long. The tail should be carried almost level with the back, and it should taper towards the point.

As the name implies, the Short-haired cat has a coat which is short, fine and close. Legs should be well built and in proportion to the body. Feet should be neat and well rounded. In fact, the general condition of a good Short-haired cat is hard and muscular, giving the appearance of activity.

If your cat answers to the above requirements a judge would allot it 50 points. He (or she) would apportion another 50 points for colour and eye-colour which differs according to the individual breeds.

Scale of Points for Structure and Condition

Body and Tail	10
Legs and Feet	5
Head and Neck	10
Ears	10
Coat	10
Condition	5
Total	50

Blue Short-hair

Like its Long-haired counterpart, the aristocrat of British Short-hairs is the Blue. It is a lovely cat. A good specimen has a light to medium-blue coat, the fur of which is short and close in texture. Provided that the coat conforms to these requirements, and there are no signs of tabby markings, white patches or shadings of any description in it, then a judge would allot the full 25 points. The remaining 25 points are allowed for the eyes. These must be large and full, and of copper, orange or yellow colour.

Breeders recommend the crossing of British Blues with Blacks, but they are strongly opposed to mating them with

Russian Blues or Blue Long-hairs. This practice was much resorted to in the past, but it often resulted in progeny with the wedge-shaped head or green eye-colour of the Russian cat, or with the long coat of the Blue Persian.

Black Short-hair

Lucky black cat! If you have a sleek, jet-black cat, with no rusty tinge or white hairs in its coat, you are fortunate indeed. If it has deep-copper or orange-coloured eyes without any trace of green, and if the eyes are large, round and well opened, it would earn a well-deserved 50 points in the show-pen.

Any black Short-haired cat is a delightful animal to possess, but one that measures up to the standard just given is exceedingly rare. In fact a really jet-black cat always has been a rarity. There was a time when such cats were kept almost exclusively by seafaring folk, sailors' wives believing that a black cat would ensure the safety of their husbands while at sea. Hence the expression 'Black cat for Luck!'

White Short-hair

This is another delightful cat. In order to win 25 points in the show-pen, however, it must be pure white, untinged with yellow. For the remaining 25 points it must have very deep sapphire-blue eyes, or golden, orange or copper eyes.

But White Short-hairs make charming pets whatever their eye-colour. Personally, I like them best with one blue and one orange eye, or one blue and one green eye. These odd-eyed cats are usually great characters.

In many ways the Short-haired White resembles the Siamese cat. It is, for example, very much a 'one-person' cat. Again, like the Siamese, it will follow you about the house and welcome you with a great show of affection every time you return from an outing. A friend of mine who keeps three Short-haired Whites tells me that one of them even sits and waits for her outside the bathroom!

Extremely intelligent, the Short-haired White is also a very hardy breed. Perhaps a little nervous of strangers, where other cats are concerned it will tolerate no interference. In fact, it will not hesitate to let them know that a Short-haired White is boss!

Cream Short-hair

For show purposes the Cream Short-hair must be rich cream, absolutely level in colour and free from bars or white patches. It must also have copper or orange-colour eyes.

Such a cat is extremely rare. Good specimens do occasionally appear at the shows, but I have yet to see one entirely without the barring. Should *you* have one, it could earn 35 points for colour and an additional 15 points for eye-colour.

Kittens are sometimes born very pale cream. Unfortunately, however, as they grow older, the barring usually makes its appearance.

Any such defect makes them no less likeable as pets.

Blue-Cream Short-hair

This is a very pretty cat indeed. In structure it resembles a British Blue cat. The coat, however, which is short and fine in texture, is blue and cream. In a good specimen the two colours are softly mingled. There should be no effect of patchiness. Eye-colour can be copper, orange or yellow, but *not* green.

Scale of Points for Blue-Cream Short-hairs

Type as for Short-haired cats	40
Colour, mingling	35
Eyes	20
Condition	5
Total	100

Tortoiseshell Short-hair

The Tortoiseshell cat has been compared to a bizarre tulip. The coat is black and red (light and dark), the colours of a good specimen being brilliant and equally balanced. There must be no white. Patches are clear and defined. There is no blurring, nor are there any tabby or brindle markings. Legs, feet, tail and ears are patched in similar fashion to the body and head. A red blaze runs up the face. If your cat answers to this description and it has orange, copper or hazel-colour eyes, then a judge would allot it 50 points.

Harrison Weir, the nineteenth-century authority on cats, described the Tortoiseshell as a triumph of art over nature. 'I deem this to be the breed wherein there is the most art and skill required to produce properly all the varied mottled beauty of bright colours. . . .'

He suggested using a Black or even a Blue male with a Yellow or Red Tabby female, and, if possible, one or both should be the progeny of a Tortoiseshell mother.

Tortoiseshell-and-White Short-hair

This is another very handsome animal. Colouring is black and red (dark and light) on white. The colours should be equally balanced, brilliant and absolutely free from brindling or tabby markings. The tricolour patches, which must be clear and well defined, should cover the top of the head, ears, cheeks, back and tail and part of flanks. If your cat measures up to this description, has a white blaze on its face, and orange, copper or hazel eyes, it would win a well-deserved 50 points.

As with their Long-haired counterparts, almost all Torties and Tortie-and-White Short-hairs are females. Probably the largest number of males ever to be seen together was in 1871, when four were exhibited at the Crystal Palace. One of these was a Tortoiseshell and the others were Tortoiseshell-and-

Whites. During the next few years several Tortie-and-White males appeared at the various cat shows. One of them became very famous indeed. It was called Totty and was valued at £100. Then, as now, however, most of the males were sterile.

Tabby Short-hairs

Tabby cats have always been popular. Varieties include the Grey Tabby, the Brown Tabby, the Red Tabby, the Silver Tabby, the Orange Tabby, the Yellow Tabby and the Mackerel Tabby. Occasionally one also meets a Blue Tabby or an Orange-and-White Tabby.

I consider the Tabby cat to be the most intelligent of all cats. As kittens they are very high spirited and always ready for a game. They can be taught to walk on a lead, to retrieve a piece of screwed-up paper or to chase a ping-pong ball. There is a very well-known Brown Tabby Short-hair which goes almost everywhere with its owner, staying with her in hotels and private houses all over Britain. One of my own Tabby Short-hairs would, voluntarily, sit up and beg like a dog.

For show purposes the Governing Council of the Cat Fancy recognises four breeds of Tabby cat. The Standard of Points for these Tabbies is as follows:

Brown Tabby Short-hairs

		POINTS
Markings	Very dense and black, not mixed with ground colour and quite distinct from it. Ground colour rich sable, or brown, uniform throughout, no white anywhere.	50
Eyes	Orange, hazel, deep yellow, or green.	

Silver Tabby Short-hairs

		POINTS
Markings	Dense black, not mixed with the ground colour and quite distinct from it. Ground colour pure, clear silver, uniform throughout, no white anywhere.	50
Eyes	Round and well opened; colour: green.	

Red Tabby Short-hairs

Markings	Very dense and dark red, not mixed with the ground colour and quite distinct from it. Ground colour and markings to be as rich red as possible.	50
Eyes	Hazel or orange.	

Mackerel-striped Tabby Short-hairs

Markings	As dense as possible, distinct from ground colour. Rings as narrow and numerous as possible, and running vertically from the spine towards the ground.	50

Note. In all Tabby cats the tails must be neatly ringed, and chest ring or rings most desirable.

Spotted Cats

Spotted cats are very attractive. Probably the best known are the Black-spotted and the Brown-spotted types, but the spots can be of any colour, so long as they are suitable to the ground colour of the cat's coat. Clear spotting is essential. A judge would not object if the spots were round, oblong or rosette-shaped, but they must be distinct and not running into each other.

Colour of eyes should conform to the coat colour. Stripes and bars, except on the face and head, would be counted as faults in the show pen. So would brindling. Judging by points, a value of 50 would be allotted to spotting, and the remaining 50 to the qualities required by other British Short-haired cats.

The Manx Cat

A Manx cat makes one of the most charming pets you could ever wish for. Affectionate and good-tempered, it is the ideal companion for children. A natural retriever, it delights in bringing back a small ball, or a piece of screwed-up paper, however many times you care to throw it. Not at all nervous, it takes readily to new surroundings and can easily be taught to walk on a lead. It has a quaint 'hoppity' gait, rather like that of a rabbit, and a shrill voice which is more like a squeak than a miaou!

Although the absence of a tail is one of the distinctive features of the Manx cat, any cat without a tail is not necessarily a Manx. In addition to complete taillessness, the true Manx cat always has a short back and high hindquarters. There is a decided hollow at the end of the backbone, where, in other cats, the tail would begin. The high rump, which should be round like an orange, is, in fact, as good a distinguishing feature as the lack of tail. There is also great depth of flank.

The Manx cat has a large and rounded head, but this does not mean that it in any way resembles the Persian cat. The ears are rather wide at the base, tapering slightly off to a point. The nose is longish and the cheeks prominent. The coat is double, being soft and open on top, like that of a rabbit, and thick and fuzzy underneath. The reason for its peculiar 'hoppity' gait is, of course, because the hind legs of the Manx are so much longer than the front ones. There is absolutely *no* truth in the absurd theory sometimes put forward that this cat is the result of a cross-mating between a cat and a rabbit.

No one knows how the Manx cat originally arrived on the Isle of Man. According to tradition some of these cats swam ashore from a Spanish ship which was wrecked near the island during the Armada. But as there are absolutely no records of tailless cats in Spain at that time, how they came to be on the ship would need some explaining!

There is another theory that the Phoenicians brought tailless cats westward from Japan in the grain boats to keep down vermin. As we certainly have evidence of tailless cats in Japan this story is feasible. But there are no traces of the migrations over those ancient trade routes of the world which they would have passed!

On the Isle of Man the tailless cat is known as a 'Rumpy', while the cat with just a few inches of tail is a 'Stumpy'. There you would find Rumpies, Stumpies and tailed cats all mixing together, so it is not unusual to get a really good Rumpy with one of the parents having a long tail, provided, of course, the tailed parent is of Manx blood.

How did the Manx cat lose its tail? One legend tells us that this tragedy happened at the time of the flood:

Noah sailing o'er the seas
Ran high and dry on Ararat.
His dog then made a spring and took
The tail from off a pussy cat.

Puss through the window quick did fly
And bravely through the waters swam,
Nor even stopped till high and dry
She landed on the Isle of Man.

This tailless puss earned Mona's thanks
And ever after was called Manx.

The first Manx to become a champion in Britain was a Silver Tabby kitten called Bonhaki, who was owned by a keeper at the London Zoo. The award was made in the presence of Queen Alexandra, then the Princess of Wales, and the show was held at the Royal Botanic Gardens. Louis Wain, the famous cat artist of those days, was judging.

You can have your Manx in black, white, tabby, red, blue, tortoiseshell – in fact, in almost any colour that you fancy, or that is obtainable at the time of purchase.

Standard of Points for Manx Cats

Taillessness, height of hindquarters, shortness of back and depth of flanks are essentials in a Manx cat, as only with them is combined the true rabbity or hopping gait. The coat is what is termed 'double', namely, soft and open like that of a rabbit, with a soft, thick undercoat. That is another essential, and great attention should be paid to roundness of rump – as round as an orange being the ideal.

SCALE OF POINTS

Taillessness	15
Height of Hindquarters	15
Shortness of Back	15
Roundness of Rump	10
Depth of Flank	10
Double Coat	10
Head and Ears	10
Colour and Markings	5
Eyes	5
Condition	5
Total	100

Remarks: Taillessness must be absolute in a show specimen. There should be a decided hollow at the end of the backbone, where in the ordinary cat the tail would begin. The hindquarters in a Manx cannot be too high, the back cannot be too short and there must be a great depth of flank. The head is round and large, but it is not a snubby or Persian type. The nose is longish, but the cheeks being very prominent do away with snipiness, which is a bad fault. The ears are rather wide at the base, tapering slightly off to a point. Eye colour is of very secondary consideration, and must be taken into account only when all other points are equal. When that is so, it follows the ideal for the British cats, namely, blue for Whites and amber or orange for Blacks, Oranges, Tortoiseshells, etc. All colours of Manx are recognised, and here again, as in eye-colour, marking and colour must be taken into account only when all other points are equal. Finally, gait, arising from the combination referred to in the opening sentence, is of primary importance.

Bi-coloured Short-hair

Colour and Distribution	Any solid colour and white, the patches of colour to be clear and evenly distributed. Not more than two thirds of the cat's coat to be coloured and not more than one half to be white. Face to be patched with colour, white blaze desirable. 25 points
Coat and Condition	Coat to be short and fine in texture. Body hard and muscular, giving a general appearance of activity. 15 points
Head	Round and broad, width between ears, which should be small and well placed. Short nose, full cheeks, wide muzzle and firm chin (level bite). 25 points
Body and Legs	Cobby, with short straight legs. 15 points
Eyes	Large and round, set well apart, deep orange, yellow or copper in colour. 15 points
Tail	Short and thick. 5 points

CHAPTER 11

FOREIGN SHORT-HAIRED CATS

SOME OF the most popular and fascinating cats are to be found among the Foreign Short-hairs. This group, which includes the Siamese, Burmese, Abyssinian, Russian Blue and Havana, is not only highly individual in character but also in appearance.

In contrast to the British Short-haired cat, the foreign type has a lissom, slender body, with a wedge-shaped head, large pointed ears and oriental almond-shaped eyes. The coat which is very short and close-lying is beautifully easy to groom. The legs are slim and dainty, while the tail is long and thin.

If you want a cat to give you a wealth of affection, then have one of these Foreign Short-hairs. Contrary to some beliefs, they are very hardy. Moreover, they are so adaptable that they will settle down with you quite happily in a town flat, a country house or cottage. Most of them are fond of travelling about with their owners and can easily be trained to walk on a lead.

Any of the Foreign Short-hairs would make an ideal companion for children, elderly people or invalids, for not only will they entertain for hours with their amusing antics, but all show a similar large measure of intelligence and faithfulness.

THE SIAMESE CAT

Outstanding among these foreign types is the Siamese, one of the most popular pedigree cats in the world. Handsome rather than pretty, the Siamese is utterly unlike any other cat in appearance, one of its most remarkable features being the face mask with coloured ears and brilliant blue eyes.

There are endless stories of the Siamese cat's intelligence and behaviour. It will follow you about the house, perch up on your shoulder, and welcome you with loud purrs after every absence, having met you at the front door after listening for the sound of your key in the lock.

Many Siamese cats know which way a door handle turns. They stand up and put their paws round the knob, turn it and push the door open. Others will beg for tit-bits like a dog.

Indeed, they have many other characteristics of the dog. They will accompany you on walks, growl over a bone, and retrieve a small stick or piece of screwed-up paper as many times as you care to throw it. But the Siamese cat is *never* servile. It will do almost anything to please you when it wants to do so, but in a perverse mood it can be as aloof and apparently self-sufficient as other types of cat. For the dog lover, a Siamese cat is *not* a substitute, both animals complement each other.

One of the Siamese cat's most interesting characteristics is its voice. This is deep, loud and husky, with many unique variations of tone. A 'talkative' pet Siamese can be an endless source of delight to its owner, but the love songs of the unneutered female in a block of flats could cause the neighbours much annoyance, to put it mildly!

The Siamese cat has inspired many legends, but the one I like best gives a touching explanation of this cat's most peculiar features, the slanted eyes and the kinked tail.

The legend tells of how two Siamese cats, Tien and Chula, went into the jungle to search for a Royal goblet that was missing from one of the temples. Upon finding the treasure they decided that Chula should remain in the jungle to guard it while Tien went back to the city to inform the priest of their discovery.

Day after day the faithful Chula watched over the precious goblet, so that eventually her lovely blue eyes began to squint. When sleep overcame her she was forced to lie down beside the treasure. But, before closing her eyes, she was careful to twist her tail round its stem to make quite certain that no one would try to take it away.

When Tien returned he found that he was the father of five beautiful kittens. In spite of her new responsibility, however, the loyal mother cat had not forgotten her earlier trust. Indeed, so conscientious had she been in her protection of the goblet, that a permanent kink had developed in the end of her tail. Moreover, all five kittens had a similar kink in their tails and their bright blue eyes squinted!

Be that as it may, squints and kinks are considered old fashioned. A prize-winning Siamese has *no* squint, although its eyes should be slanted. And although a tiny kink in the end of the tail is permissible, a long straight tail is just as Royal.

Siamese cats first appeared in Britain in 1884, and were exhibited at the Crystal Palace a year later. In 1901 the Siamese Cat Club was founded, which is now the largest specialist club in Europe. There are also several other clubs devoted to the interests of Siamese cats, including the Siamese Cat Society of the British Empire, the Siamese Cat Association and the Northern Siamese Cat Society.

At the time of writing there are eight recognised breeds of Siamese cat in Britain. In pattern, texture of coat, shape of body and length of tail they are all identical. All have the same type of long, wedge-shaped head, with large pricked ears and slanted eyes. It is only in colour that they differ.

Who does not know the Seal-Pointed Siamese with its lovely cream and fawn coat? The points, which are mask, ears, legs, feet and tail, are dark seal-brown. Eyes are a brilliant deep blue.

Almost as popular as the Seal-Point is the Blue-Pointed variety. This cat has a glacial-white coat shading to silvery-blue on the back, the points being a slightly darker shade of blue. Then there is the Chocolate-Pointed Siamese, which has an ivory-coloured coat and points the colour of milk chocolate. The Lilac-Pointed Siamese is another almost white cat but it has delicate frost-grey points.

One of the most spectacular of the newer Siamese cats is the Red-Pointed variety. A good specimen has a white coat, shading to apricot on the back, while the ears, mask, feet and tail are bright reddish gold. The eyes are vivid blue, contrasting beautifully with the red points.

The Tabby-Pointed Siamese has a pale coat with clearly defined stripes on the mask and legs, and a neatly ringed tail. As the name implies, the Tortie-Pointed cat has tortoise-shell point colouring, and is almost always female.

Any Other Colour Siamese include cats with cream points, lilac-cream points, chocolate-cream points and blue-cream points, as well as other unusual colours.

Siamese kittens are born white, the colour gradually appearing on the ears and tail within a few days. A little later the colour develops on the mask, legs and paws. By the time the cat is an adult the mask should be complete, when it is then connected by tracings with the ears.

You can never fool a Siamese cat. Punish it unfairly and it will ignore you. Give it your friendship and it will give handsomely in return. But do remember that a Siamese cat *must* have human companionship, so please do not have one unless you are prepared to give it a little of your time. Almost always it is a 'one-person' cat, and while it will cheerfully tolerate every member of the household, it reserves its most endearing ways for the human that it owns.

Standard of Points for the Seal-Pointed Siamese

Shape (Body and Tail)	Medium in size, body long and svelte, legs proportionately slim, hind legs slightly higher than the front ones, feet small and oval, tail long and tapering (either straight or slightly kinked at the extremity). The body, legs, feet, head and tail all in proportion, giving the whole a well-balanced appearance.

Head and Ears	Head long and well proportioned, with width between the eyes, narrowing in perfectly straight lines to a fine muzzle. Ears rather large and pricked, wide at the base.
Eyes (Colour and Shape)	Clear, brilliant deep blue. Shape oriental and slanting towards the nose. No tendency to squint.
Body Colour	Cream shading gradually into pale warm fawn on the back. Kittens paler in colour.
Points	Mask, ears, legs, feet and tail dense and clearly defined seal-brown. Mask complete and (except in kittens) connected by tracings with the ears.
Coat	Very short and fine in texture, glossy and close-lying.

Notes and Definitions

Definition of Squint	When the eyes are so placed that they appear to look permanently at the nose.

Notes. The Siamese Cat should be a beautifully balanced animal with head, ears and neck carried on a long svelte body, supported on fine legs and feet with a tail in proportion. The head and profile should be wedge-shaped, neither round nor pointed. The mask complete connected by tracings with the ears (except in kittens), the eyes a deep blue, green tinge to be considered a fault. Expression alert and intelligent.

White toes or toe to automatically disqualify an exhibit. It is important to note that the Standard with regard to Type and Shape is the same for all Siamese Cats.

SCALE OF POINTS

Type and Shape

Head	15	
Ears	5	25
Eyes	5	
Body	15	
Legs and Paws	5	25
Tail	5	
	Total	50

Colour

Eyes	15	
Points	10	35
Body Colour	10	
Texture of Coat	10	15
Condition	5	
	Total	50

Siamese (Blue-Pointed)

The standard is the same as for Seal-Pointed with the following exceptions:

Colour Points blue, the ears, mask, legs, paws and tail to be the same colour. The ears should not be darker than the other points.

Eyes Clear, bright, vivid blue.

Body Body colour, glacial-white, shading gradually into blue on the back, the same cold tone as the points but of a lighter shade.

Texture of Coat The same as for Seal-Pointed.

Siamese (Chocolate-Pointed)

The standard is the same as for Seal-Pointed with the following exceptions:

Colour	Points milk chocolate, the ears, mask, legs, paws and tail to be the same colour, the ears should not be darker than the other points.
Eyes	Clear, bright, vivid blue.
Body	Ivory colour all over. Shading, if at all, to be to colour of points.
Texture of Coat	The same as for Seal-Pointed.

Siamese (Lilac-Pointed)

The standard is the same as for Seal-Pointed with the following exceptions:

Eyes	Clear, light, vivid blue.
Points	Pinkish grey.
Nose Leather and Pads	Faded lilac.
Body Colour	Off-white (magnolia) shading, if any, to tone with points.
Texture of Coat	As for all Siamese.

Number of points to be awarded for any feature to be the same as for all Siamese.

The Abyssinian Cat

Although still one of the rarer breeds, the Abyssinian Cat is definitely becoming more popular. This is not surprising, for it is an extremely affectionate breed, elegant in appearance and full of character. There are those who claim that it has much in common with the Siamese cat. Certainly, it will follow its owner like a dog, can be trained to walk on a lead and has a natural instinct for retrieving. But the Abyssinian has a much quieter voice than the Siamese, in fact, it is much more like that of the 'ordinary' cat.

Why the Abyssinian gets its name is something of a mystery, for the breed was never prolific in that part of Africa. Most Abyssinian owners like to believe that their cats are the nearest approach to the Egyptian Sacred Cat, and it cannot be denied that the present-day Abyssinian bears a close resemblance to the drawings and carvings of that animal.

Every Egyptian householder of any standing kept one, which came under the protection of Pasht, Goddess of the Moon. When one of these cats died it was given an elaborate funeral, the owner shaving off his eyebrows as an expression of grief.

Nobody was allowed to kill a cat, and it was said that Cambyses, King of the Medes and Persians, won a victory over the Egyptians by giving each of his soldiers a live cat to hold instead of a shield. He was alleged to have known that the Egyptians would never shoot at them.

Be that as it may, the first Abyssinian cat to arrive in Britain did come from Abyssinia. It belonged to a Mrs Barrett-Lennard and was called Zula. A reference to it occurs in Dr Gordon Staples' *Cats, Their Points*, etc. (1874), and tells of how it was fed on raw beef and for a long time was very wild.

> 'She is now very fond of her mistress, but has a great many eccentricities which other cats have not, and is altogether a wonderful specimen of cat-kind.'

At early cat shows the Abyssinian appeared to be the cause of much confusion, and was exhibited under a number of different names. These included the Hare and Rabbit cat, the Abyssinian Silver-Grey cat, and even the Chinchilla Abyssinian. Larger than our modern species, nevertheless, we are given to understand that it was a very graceful cat. Harrison Weir describes it in *Our Cats and All About Them*

(1889), as deep brown in colour, ticked with black, 'somewhat resembling the back of a wild (only not so grey) rabbit'.

The Abyssinian as we know it is a small cat and very pretty. It has a long and pointed head, but not so long or as pointed as that of the Siamese. It has large pointed ears, and very expressive almond-shaped eyes, which may be green, yellow or hazel. On first sight it could just be taken for a Tabby, but on closer inspection one realises that there are absolutely *no* tabby markings. The coat is, in fact, a beautiful shade of russet brown.

The fur, which is short and silky, is close in texture and shows double or treble ticking. In other words, each hair has two or three bands of colour, shading from reddish-brown to black or darker brown. The forelegs and stomach are reddish-brown to harmonise with the main colour.

A recent development in the Abyssinian Cat Fancy has been the breeding of Red Abyssinians. These have every characteristic of the better known Abyssinian cat except colour which is rich copper red, doubly or trebly ticked with darker colours.

Standard of Points for the Abyssinian

Colour and Type	Ruddy brown, ticked with black or dark brown, double or treble ticking – i.e. two or three bands of colour on each hair preferable to single ticking; no bars or other markings except that a dark spine line will not militate against an otherwise good specimen. Inside of fore-legs and belly should be of a tint to harmonise well with the main colour, the preference being given to orange-brown.
Absence of Markings	i.e. bars on head, tail, face and chest – is a very important property in this breed. These places are just where, if a cat or other feline animal shows markings at all, they will hold

their ground to the last with remarkable pertinacity. The less markings visible the better; at the same time the judge must not attach such undue importance to this property that he fails to give due importance to others. For instance, it does not follow that an absolutely unmarked cat, but of 'cobby' build, failing in ticking and colour is, on account of absence of marking, better than a cat of slender build, well ticked, and of nice colour, but handicapped by a certain amount of 'barring' on legs and tail.

Head and Ears	Head to be a medium wedge of heart-shaped proportions, ears sharp, comparatively large and broad at base.
Eyes	Large, bright and expressive. Colour: Green, yellow or hazel.
Tail	Fairly long and tapering.
Feet	Small, pads black; this colour also extending up the back of hind legs.
Coat	Short, fine and close.
Size	Never large or coarse.

SCALE OF POINTS

Colour		
Body Colour	30	50
Ticking	20	
Type		
Head and Ears	15	50
Eyes	5	
Body shape, tail, feet coat and carriage	20	
General Condition	10	
Total		100

Note. Although imperfect cats may be awarded prizes according to the merit of the entry, no Abyssinian should be awarded a champion certificate that has distinct bars and rings on legs and tail, white chin to be considered undesirable, other white markings not permissible.

The Russian Blue

Another attractive and very friendly breed is the Russian Blue. A good specimen has a lithe and graceful body, a flat, narrow head, large pointed ears and almond-shaped, vivid green eyes. The coat is really lovely, a pure unmarked blue. Short, close-lying and lustrous, it differs from that of any other cat, blue or otherwise.

The Russian Blue is alleged to be a very ancient breed which can be traced back to the days of the Vikings. According to the following lines from an old Russian prayer, blue cats certainly were not uncommon in that country:

> Hear our prayer, Lord, for all animals,
> May they be well-fed and well-treated and happy:
> Protect them from hunger and fear and suffering:
> And, we pray, protect specially, dear Lord,
> The little blue cat who is the companion of our home.
> Keep her safe as she goes abroad
> And bring her back to comfort us.
>
> *Translated by Ian Deverit-Bennett*

One of the first Russian Blue cats to arrive in Britain is thought to have been the gift of a Russian Tsar to an English diplomat. During the nineteenth century many other fine specimens made their appearance, and it is said that one such cat was handed to a docker by a Russian sailor in exchange for a leg of mutton!

In those days the Russian Blue was known as the Archangel Cat, and it had fiery yellow eyes. At early shows it was also exhibited under such names as Blue Russian, Foreign Blue, Spanish Blue, and yes, even American Blue! There were breeders who refused to believe that it was a new variety and persisted in crossing it with the British Blue. Naturally, this did much to spoil both breeds, as well as causing even more confusion.

By 1948, however, matters had taken a turn for the better. This was entirely due to a small band of loyal and very skilful breeders, and as a result of their efforts the Russian Blue was once again established as a separate breed.

Of one thing you may be certain, the Russian Blue makes a delightful and very hardy pet. It is capable of the same high degree of intelligence and devotion whether or not its ancestors ever saw the palace of a Tsar!

Standard of Points for Russian Blue Short-hairs

Colour	Clear blue, even throughout, and in maturity free from tabby markings or shading. Medium blue is preferred.
Coat	Short, thick and very fine, standing up soft and silky like seal skin. Very different from any other breed. Coat is double so that it has a distinct, silvery sheen. The texture and appearance of the coat is the truest criterion of the Russian Blue.
Body	Body long and graceful in outline and carriage. Medium strong bone.
Tail	Tail fairly long and tapering.
Legs and feet	Legs long, feet small and oval.
Head	Short wedge, with flat skull; forehead and nose straight, forming an angle. Prominent whisker pads.
Eyes	Vivid green, set rather wide apart, almond in shape.
Ears	Large and pointed, wide at base and set vertically to the head. Skin of ears thin and transparent, with very little inside furnishing.

Faults White or tabby markings. Cobby or heavy build. Square head. Yellow in eyes. Siamese type is undesirable.

SCALE OF POINTS

Colour	20
Coat and Condition	25
Body, Build & Tail	25
Eyes	15
Head and Ears	15
Total	100

Burmese

Burmese cats are among the most popular of the Foreign Short-haired types. There are several recognised varieties, but the best known are the Brown and the Blue. As their names imply, the Brown Burmese has a dark, seal-brown coat, while the Blue Burmese has a silver-grey coat. Eyes are yellow.

Other varieties include the Cream, Red, Blue-Cream, Chocolate (also known as the Champagne), Lilac and Tortoiseshell Burmese. All are medium-sized cats, with long, lissom bodies on long, slim legs. All have a similar type of wedge-shaped head and relatively large ears, which are wide at the base and slightly rounded at the tips. All have a fairly long and slightly tapering tail. It is only in the matter of colour that they differ.

Burmese Cats came to Britain from America, where they were introduced about 1930 by Dr Joseph Thompson of San Francisco, who brought a pair back with him from the Far East. These first specimens, however, were not Burmese Cats as we know them, but Burmese–Siamese hybrids. One of them was called Wong-Mau.

Later, further breeding stock was secured through the Harvard School of Genetics by an eminent American cat fancier, Mr Donald Came. It was he who first produced the cat we now recognise as the Burmese.

The first Burmese Cats to arrive in Britain were two females and a male – Chindwins Minou Twm, Laos Cheli Wat and Casa Gatos Da Foong. These were all brown cats and were imported soon after the last war by Mr and Mrs Sidney France of Derby. In 1953, through the interest and help of the late Lord Aberconway, another Burmese male (also a brown one) crossed the Atlantic. This cat, Casa Gatos Darkee, was destined to become very famous. For not only did he achieve a championship and sire champions, but he also sired the first Blue Burmese ever to be born in Britain – namely, Sealcoat Blue Surprise.

Soon it was discovered that certain Brown Burmese carried a factor for blue, and if two such cats were mated they could produce *some* blue kittens. When a Blue Burmese was later mated to a brown cat carrying the blue factor, a larger number of blue kittens could be produced. But neither of these matings could produce an entire litter of blue kittens – for this Blue needed to be mated to Blue.

The first all-Blue litter of Burmese kittens appeared in April 1958, and by the end of that year four such Blue litters from Blue Burmese parents had been born. In July 1960 this attractive variety was officially recognised by the Governing Council of the Cat Fancy, and granted a breed number, 27A. Since then, the newer colour-varieties have been evolved as a result of selective breeding.

Standard of Points for Burmese

Body, Legs and Tail The body should be of medium length and size, feeling hard and muscular, and heavier than its appearance indicates. The chest should be strong, and rounded in profile, the back straight from shoulder to rump. Legs should be slender and in proportion to the body; hind legs slightly longer than front: paws neat and oval in shape. The tail should be straight and of medium length, not heavy at base, and tapering only slightly to a rounded tip without bone defect. A visible kink or other bone defect in the tail is a fault, precluding the award of a challenge certificate, but an invisible defect at the extreme tip may be overlooked in an otherwise excellent specimen.

Head, Ears and Eyeset The head should be slightly rounded on top, with good breadth between the ears, having wide cheek bones and tapering to a short blunt wedge. The jaw should be wide at the hinge and the chin firm. A muzzle pinch is a bad fault. Ears should be medium in size, set well apart on the skull, broad at the base, with slightly rounded tips, the outer line of the ears continuing the shape of the upper part of the face. This may not be possible in mature males who develop a fullness of cheek. In profile the ears should be seen to have a slight forward tilt. There should be a distinct nose break, and in profile the chin should show a strong lower jaw. The eyes, which must be set well apart, should be large and lustrous, the top line of the eye showing a straight oriental slant towards the nose, the lower line being rounded. Either round or oriental eyes are a fault.

Eye Colour	Eyes should be any shade of yellow from chartreuse to amber, with golden yellow preferred. Green eyes are a serious fault in Brown Burmese, but Blue Burmese may show a slight fading of colour. Green eyes with more blue than yellow pigmentation must preclude the award of a challenge certificate in all coloured Burmese.
Coat	The coat should be short, fine, satin-like in texture, lying close to the body. The glossy coat is a distinctive feature of Burmese and is indicative of good health.
Condition	Cats should be well-muscled, with good weight for size: lively and alert.

SCALE OF POINTS

Body shape, legs, tail, feet	30
Body colour, coat texture and condition	25
Head and ears	20
Shape and set of eyes	15
Colour of eyes	10
	100

The above distribution of points applies to all Burmese cats except the Tortie varieties.

Havana

The Havana (previously called the Chestnut Brown Foreign) is a chestnut-brown cat with oriental-shaped green eyes. Although of foreign type, it is a product of British breeders, the initial matings having been made with black cats, Chocolate-Pointed Siamese and Russian Blues.

For some years this cat was known as the Chestnut Brown Foreign in Britain. In 1970, however, it was re-christened the Havana, the name by which it has always been known in Continental Europe and the USA.

The Havana is a very graceful cat. Lithe and sinuous, it has a long, well-proportioned head and large, pointed ears. The legs are slim and dainty, with hind legs slightly higher than the front ones. The tail is long and whip-like, and there should be no kink. The coat is short and glossy.

Havanas are very intelligent and affectionate. The females make good mothers and are fairly prolific breeders, litters ranging from about five to seven.

Standard of Points for the Havana

Havana Cats are of foreign type. They are fine in bone, lithe and sinuous and of graceful proportions. The coat is a rich brown, even and sound, whiskers and nose to be of the same colour as the coat. The pads of the feet are a pinkish shade. The eyes are green.

Coat	Any shade of rich chestnut-brown, short and glossy, even and sound throughout.
Head and Ears	Head long and well proportioned, narrowing to a fine muzzle, ears large and pricked, wide at the base with good width between.
Body, Legs and Tail	Body long, lithe and well muscled, graceful in outline. Legs slim and dainty, hind legs slightly higher than front legs. Paws oval and neat. Long whip tail, no kink.
Eyes	Slanting and Oriental in shape, decidedly green in colour.

SCALE OF POINTS

Coat	30
Head	15
Body	15
Legs	15
Tail	5
Eyes	10
Condition	10
Total	100

Foreign White

This is a very attractive cat indeed. Of Siamese type and temperament, it has a snow-white coat with no contrasting colour on the points. Its slanting, oriental eyes are sapphire blue.

It was originally produced by mating Short-haired white cats with Siamese, then repeatedly back-crossing the best of the white progeny to Seal-Pointed Siamese of excellent type. It has all the characteristics of the Siamese cat, including the husky voice and wonderful devotion to its owners. Furthermore, unlike many other white cats, it is never deaf.

Foreign Lilac

Also known as the Foreign Lavender, Self-Lilac or Self-Lavender, this is yet another cat which has been derived from the Siamese, in this case the Lilac-Pointed variety. It has a short, soft coat which, in a good specimen, is pale lilac or pale lavender all over. Eye-colour is a vivid shade of apple green. Intelligent and affectionate, it is becoming deservedly very popular.

Korat

Although this cat was introduced to Britain from the USA in 1972, the breed is not native to that country. It traces its ancestry back to North-eastern Thailand, where it is regarded as an omen of good luck!

The Korat is a beautiful cat. Of medium size, with silver-blue fur, it has a heart-shaped face, large ears and very expressive green eyes. Gentle and playful, it becomes very devoted to its owners.

The American Korat Cat Fanciers Association, from which the British imports were obtained, is determined to keep the breed absolutely pure, and undoubtedly British fanciers will do the same.

CHAPTER 12

REX CATS

When Rex cats were first exhibited at the Kensington Kitten Show in 1956, they were considered something of a novelty. Today, these fascinating animals are so popular that they deserve a chapter to themselves.

The Rex is quite unlike any other cat in that it has a wavy coat. There are two varieties, the Cornish and the Devon, and there is quite a lot of difference between them.

Both are medium-sized cats with slender bodies carried high on long, slim legs, and both have long, tapering tails. But whereas the Cornish has a longish head with a straight profile, the Devon has what might be described as a pixie-like face. That is to say, it has a shorter head, full cheeks and a 'whisker-break'. In profile, its nose shows a definite 'stop'.

Both types of Rex cat have short, wavy coats, but that of the Cornish is thick and plushy, while the Devon's is finer and soft. If a Cornish Rex is to win a prize in a show, its fur must be deeply waved or corrugated, and these ripples must cover its entire body, particularly its back and tail. Even its whiskers and eyebrows are curly.

Rex cats are bred in almost every colour and coat pattern including black, white, red, grey, blue, smoke, blue-cream, tortoiseshell and tabby. You can also have your Rex with a Siamese coat pattern. It is known as the Si-Rex, and can be of Cornish or Devon type.

Both the Cornish and the Devon Rex have large ears and oval-shaped eyes. But while the ears of the Cornish are set rather high on the head, those of the Devon are set rather low. Also, the eyes of the Devon are larger and more slanting. Eye-colour of both cats should be in keeping with the coat pattern.

The first Rex cat ever to be discovered in Britain was a ginger-and-white male named Kallibunker. Born in 1950 on a Cornish farm, he was a mutation in a litter of ordinary straight-coated kittens. So impressed was the owner by the waves and crinkles in this unusual kitten's coat, that she showed him to her vet, who suggested that she should get in touch with an expert on cat genetics.

This resulted in Kallibunker being mated back to his mother (an ordinary tortoiseshell-and-white cat), when a litter of two kittens with wavy coats and one with a plain coat was born. Later, when this mating was repeated, further wavy-coated kittens were produced. Unfortunately, Kallibunker died, but he left some wavy-coated sons to carry on the breeding programme.

Even so, fresh blood was necessary if the kittens' stamina was to be maintained. Therefore, it was decided to out-cross one of the wavy-coated males to an ordinary straight-coated female. The result of this union was a litter of plain-coated kittens. When these were mated back to their sire, however, or to each other, a percentage of wavy-coated kittens was produced in every litter.

Meanwhile, zoologists and cat fanciers were taking a great interest in this unusual cat's progress. Photographs began to appear in the newspapers and magazines carrying such captions as 'Something Different in the Cat World', or 'The Cat Everyone Has Been Waiting to See'. Often it was referred to as the 'Poodle Cat', having, as one writer described it, 'curly fur that is soft beyond belief'.

Then, in 1960, another wavy-coated cat was discovered, this time in Devon. His name was Kirlee. Since this new Rex cat came from a neighbouring county to that of the original Kallibunker, breeders naturally assumed that the animals were related. Imagine their disappointment when Kirlee was mated to one of Kallibunker's descendants, only for an entire litter of plain-coated kittens to be born. Neither did repeated matings give any different results.

The only thing to do was to follow a similar breeding programme to the one that had proved so successful with Kallibunker. Unfortunately, Kirlee's mother was dead, so one of his daughters was mated back to him. Once again, a percentage of wavy-coated kittens was produced.

The conclusion was obvious. There are two distinct types of Rex cat – one descended from the Cornish Kallibunker and the other from the Devon Kirlee. In 1967 both types were officially recognised by the Governing Council of the Cat Fancy, and a standard of points for each was drawn up. It was decided to call them Rex cats because of the similarity of their coats to that of the Astrex rabbit.

Rex cats make delightful pets. Intelligent and affectionate, they get on well with children and dogs, are easy to house-train and can be taught to walk on a lead. In spite of having only one layer to their coats, instead of the normal three (a soft undercoat, middle coat and guard hairs), they are extremely hardy. Mrs Alison Ashford, an enthusiastic breeder of both types of Rex, tells me that her cats go out in all but the frostiest weather. 'But,' she warns, 'a rain-shower soon soaks them as their coats are not water-resistant.'

Rex cats never moult, so they are very easy to groom. Unless you intend to show your pet, hand-grooming with a slightly moist hand is usually all that is required. It is also advisable to wipe round the inner corners of your cat's eyes occasionally, and to clean his ears very gently, as suggested in Chapter 2.

If you do want to show your cat, then a little more beauty treatment is necessary. This especially applies to the white Rex, which should be bathed in luke-warm water the evening before the show. Use a mild baby shampoo and, after rinsing, be sure to dry him thoroughly. Don't let him out or he may catch a chill. Give him a drink of warm milk.

All cats need a well-balanced diet, and the Rex is no exception. It thrives on meat, fish, rabbit, milk and cereal but, having no guard hairs, it loses more body heat than other cats. Therefore, it is advisable to mix a small amount of vegetable oil into one of its meals daily. Soya or corn oil would be suitable.

Mention must be made of the Rex cat's passion for exotic foods. Most of them show great delight if offered small pieces of Stilton cheese, smoked salmon or milk chocolate. While such tasty morsels cannot be recommended as part of your cat's regular diet, there is no reason why it should not be indulged occasionally.

CHAPTER 13

WHAT MAKES A PRIZE-CAT?

MORE AND more cat lovers are getting caught up in 'Show Fever'. This is as it should be, for healthy competition not only helps to raise the standard of the various breeds, but also the welfare of the cat generally.

What makes a prize-cat?

If it is a pedigree, naturally, it must conform to the standard of points for its breed. While it is doubtful if any cat possesses *all* the qualities which make for perfection, the prize-winners do approach near to that ideal.

To readers who have never exhibited a cat, but wish to do so, I would suggest first attending several shows as a visitor. Look at all the exhibits of the same breed as your own cat, and try to assess whether it has a chance against the prize-winners. If you can bring yourself to be sufficiently critical (naturally, we all think of our own cats as perfect!) you will be surprised how fascinating and rewarding such comparisons can be.

Before you go to the shows, however, do be sure to study the standard of points required for your breed. This will be found in the chapter devoted to your own breed.

Suppose your cat falls far short of the breed standard? Do not waste your entry fees. Buy it a companion. And, when choosing your new kitten, make quite sure to tell the breeder that you want one which is up to championship show standard. A reputable breeder will not sell you an inferior kitten.

Even so, your cat may not win at its first show, and it may not win at every show. Much depends upon condition and the way it is presented. Consistent prize-winners are groomed from early kittenhood. This not only means that the coat is always at its best, but accustoms the animal to being handled. A struggling cat certainly does not make the judge's work any easier.

Suggestions for show preparation were made in an earlier chapter, but the methods of successful exhibitors may help. Mrs Joan Stuart, whose beautiful Silver Tabby Short-hair, Premier Culverden Gerard, has won many prizes including 'Best Neuter in Show', brushes him sometimes twice a day. She uses a fairly hard brush with close bristles – 'My cat is strong and heavily-built, and likes hard brushing.' After brushing, his owner rubs him down with a silk handkerchief, stroking towards the tail and down the legs.

'Ears are frequently inspected, and kept clean by wiping out with cotton wool, but they are also examined regularly by a veterinary surgeon, who also looks at his teeth. These collect tartar and should be scaled when required.'

Miss E. E. Sellars, whose Long-haired Blue-Cream, Champion Pilgrim Mayflower, won her championship in three consecutive shows, also stresses the importance of regular and consistent grooming. 'Combs and brushes are always kept handy,' she says, 'and by doing a little at a time, neither you nor the cats get tired.'

Both Champion Pilgrim Mayflower and Miss Sellars' Long-haired Cream neuter, Premier Pilgrim Giglet, live in the house with her and get plenty of affection and human company. They are given a varied diet which includes raw meat, fish and poultry, for good food is, of course, another essential if a cat is to keep in good condition.

No judge likes to handle a spiteful cat, and you will find that almost all the prize-winners have a reputation for being exceptionally gentle and affectionate. Many of them even enjoy the shows, and welcome the attention of the judges, stewards and members of the public.

This matter of temperament is as much due to a cat's ancestry as are show points. Indeed, this is another reason for making quite sure that any future show cat has a good breeding history on both sides.

Of course, no cat should be shown continually, however excellent its appearance. Kittens especially must be rested between shows, otherwise their growth may be hindered and loss of condition will result. Moreover, no kitten should ever be shown unless it has been immunised against Feline Infectious Enteritis. The second injection should be given not later than fourteen days before the show date.

Newcomers to the show world will find that the various cat clubs are always willing to give helpful information and advice. These clubs are listed in Chapter 4, which also gives details on showing. The Feline Advisory Bureau, particulars of which are given in the chapter on cat welfare, also issues very helpful and informative leaflets on show procedure and preparation.

Finally, no beginner need ever hesitate to seek the advice of more experienced exhibitors, stewards or judges. But do be sure to approach such people at a convenient time, and never before the judging is over.

CHAPTER 14

THE CAT IN YOUR HOME

IS IT a soft, silky creature that purrs gently, rubbing and coiling round your legs in anticipation of food? Or, is it a furry bundle of mischief who appears to be completely self-reliant?

No one can generalise about cats to any great extent because they are all so highly individual. Nevertheless, the more time we spend with these fascinating animals the better we understand them.

There are cats who love to be stroked (always stroke firmly but gently, and never against the grain), and are always demanding affection. They adore to be tickled behind the ears and under the jaws, and will roll over on their backs and look up at you as if in appreciation of your attention. But there are also a large number of cats who, although very happy to be with you, will not tolerate petting of any description.

Some cats never stray far from the home – I know one who rarely leaves his own small garden. On the other hand, there are others (yes, even neuters) who think nothing of forsaking the most devoted owner for several days at a time. When they return they receive a tremendous welcome. They eat a good meal, then settle down again without giving a care as to all the worry they have caused!

The fact is that cats continually keep us guessing. But is not that part of their great charm? Think of the way they lie purring contentedly in your lap. Then, suddenly, they jump away and set about washing themselves with frenzied determination. Has your lap become too warm? Your knees too hard? It is impossible to know. What is quite certain, however, is that for the moment they prefer their own company.

One of the cat's chief attractions is its poise and tranquillity. You may smile at the idea of a cat teaching us to take life calmly, but it can. Watch how elegantly your own cat sits, back slighty curved, head erect, and the hind legs wrapped by the supple tail. Observe the lovely shapes it falls into when asleep, a favourite one being the curled-up position with paws tucked under the head. The way it yawns and stretches on waking. . . .

An outstanding cat trait is, of course, its cleanliness. Nevertheless, it is not out of vanity that a cat licks itself (washing is an inaccurate term), but due to its original way of living. For the cat hunts by stealth and licks its fur to be free of tell-tale odour.

Some cats are much more fastidious over the business of washing than others. There are even a few who will skip washing altogether for a while. Generally speaking, however, a cat which is in the habit of keeping itself clean, but then suddenly neglects to do so, is ailing, and you should have veterinary advice.

Most cats are 'talkative', but the sound they appear to reserve especially for humans is the MIAOU. There are many different miaous, from the pleasant PRRAEOU sound of greeting, to the strident MRRAOU or demand for food. One of my cats always gave a polite MIEU whenever he was about to jump on to my lap. He also gave a shorter, softer MEU if, say, he was curled up in my armchair and I stopped to pat him in passing by.

Gently stroke a cat's head and probably it will start to purr. There are cats who purr almost every time you touch or speak to them. No one knows for certain how a cat produces its purr although various theories have been put forward. The most probable of these, in my opinion, is that the cat possesses some membranes or vocal cords which are subsidiary to the true vocal cords, and these are used especially for purring.

Cats are very clever at climbing and jumping. They have been known to fall unhurt from heights that would almost certainly have killed another animal or human. Nevertheless, in spite of their remarkable muscular control and flexibility, they do not always land on their feet. Even when they do, there is always the danger of internal injury. If your cat is unfortunate enough to have a fall, do get the vet to examine it. Personally, I do *not* believe that cats have nine lives.

Nor is it true that cats can see in the dark, although they *can* see better than other animals in comparative darkness. The reason is that the surface of a cat's eye is exceptionally large in proportion to the size and weight of its body. Moreover, the pupils, being highly sensitive, are able to contract to a narrow slit whenever they are exposed to strong light, and to expand (rather like the aperture of a camera lens) in darkness. Carl Van Vechten tells us that in China it has sometimes been the fashion to tell the time of day by looking at the eyes of a cat.

Almost equally helpful to a cat are its whiskers. These act as feelers, each one consisting of highly sensitive nerves. Through its whiskers a cat senses danger. When hunting, for example, it is able to keep its eyes fixed firmly on the prey, relying upon its whiskers to guide it past obstacles.

Cats also use their whiskers to carry out investigations. They will often sniff at a strange object and then explore it more fully with their whisker-tips. Many cats also make each other's acquaintance by touching whiskers.

Your cat is not always angry whenever it moves its tail. Indeed, a gently waving tail is a sign of affection. It is the thrashing of the tail from side to side which denotes anger. When your cat comes in from the garden with tail straight out and the fur upstanding, then it has probably been on a hunting expedition and is still in a state of excitement. When it strolls away from you with tail raised at right angles to its back, it is showing complete indifference. A cat of my own would act in this manner if, for example, I was at my desk typing and compelled to refuse it a lap!

A tail curled against the body means that your cat is frightened. A twitching tail-tip signifies curiosity.

Another familiar habit of the cat is to arch its back, and this it does almost whenever it encounters an unfriendly dog. Up goes the back, the hairs on it stand erect, while swear words are hissed, growled or spat at the enemy. The arched back always indicates a fighting attitude, the muscles being contracted and ready for use. The hairs of the coat normally lie at an angle to the skin, but are made to stand upright when the nerves and muscles are tensed for action.

Cats are very sensitive to weather conditions, most of them feeling real discomfort at the approach of a storm. This, of course, may have something to do with the electricity in the atmosphere and that in the cat's fur. Personally, however, I refuse to believe old superstitions such as if a cat turns its tail to the fire there will be a hard frost, or if a cat sneezes rain will follow!

CHAPTER 15

FAMOUS CAT LOVERS

THROUGHOUT THE ages many famous men and women have delighted in the companionship of cats. The friendship of great statesmen has been devoted to these creatures, writers have paid homage to them in poetry and prose, while many actors, artists, dancers and musicians have favoured them as pets.

Cardinal Richelieu was such a great cat lover that he found it impossible to work unless there were several kittens playing on his desk. One day when he was entertaining the ambassador of a neighbouring country he apologised to his guest for not rising to greet him, for, as he explained, it would have meant disturbing the mother cat and her kittens, which were all nestling comfortably in his robe. On another occasion an old lady came to ask the Cardinal for a pension. She explained that she also kept a cat, and was given an extra £20 for its keep. When the Cardinal heard that this cat had just given birth to a family of kittens he produced yet a further sum of money to buy milk.

King Louis XV of France owned a beautiful white Angora cat which was renowned for its gentle behaviour. This cat was provided with a special crimson cushion in front of the fire in the Council Chamber at Versailles, and there it slept contentedly for hours. There came a day, however, when King Louis entered the room to find his cat in a very bad temper indeed. Its back was hunched and it was swearing and spitting at his courtiers.

So unexpected was this strange behaviour on the part of his usually docile pet that Louis determined to find out the reason. He questioned a young man called Champenetz, who tried to make a joke of the matter. Eventually, however, finding that the King was serious, he confessed: 'Your Majesty's courtiers have been teasing the cat. In fact they have been throwing scent over it.' The King was furious. 'Gentlemen,' he said, 'I leave you now.' Then in a voice not to be misunderstood: 'If you wish to amuse yourselves again, remember it is *not* to be at the expense of my cat.'

The King's wishes were respected, and the cat was never teased again.

Another French cat lover was Chateaubriand, famous writer of Napoleon's time. When he was living in Rome he was presented with a cat called Micetto. It was a gift from Pope Leo XII, another great cat lover. He took it back with him to Paris, where it became a great companion. Later, when Chateaubriand was exiled in London, he lodged with an Irish landlady who was also devoted to cats. Their common love of these animals did much to ease his loneliness.

Cardinal Wolsey was an ardent admirer of cats, and whenever he received anyone in audience there was at least one cat to be seen curled up on the arm of his chair. Monsieur Poincaré favoured the Siamese cat, and he, too, was rarely without one of these creatures sleeping by his side. He once returned a neighbour's Siamese, which had taken a great fancy to him, with the words: 'He did me the honour to like me.'

Dr Johnson's fondness for cats is well known. Did he not buy oysters for Hodge, his favourite cat? James Boswell tells of the Doctor's anger on hearing of a young man who was in the habit of shooting cats. Determined to protect his own cat from such a fate, he declared: 'Hodge shan't be shot; no, no, Hodge shan't be shot.'

Théophile Gautier adored all cats. He described them as 'delightful, quiet, mysterious, gentle animals . . .'. He kept many cats himself, a favourite being Madame Théophile, a reddish cat with a white shirt-front. This cat was claimed to be so fond of music that she could distinguish good singing from bad. Therefore, if she heard a note that was pitched too high she would place a dainty paw over the singer's mouth to silence the displeasing sound!

Samuel Butler was a great friend of all stray cats. 'I must have a cat whom I find homeless,' he wrote. William Cowper had a passion for all cats, but seemed particularly interested in one which was in the habit of jumping on to his lap and then climbing up and biting the hair from his temples! Wordsworth was a cat lover and wrote poems about them. So did Thomas Hardy and Walter de la Mare. When Hardy's cat died he vowed, as many of us have done, that he would never have another pet rather than have to face the ordeal of losing it again. Mark Twain was convinced that a home was found wanting without a well-fed and well-petted cat. Matthew Arnold compared his cat to a Roman Emperor.

W. H. Davies was fond of dogs and cats. Do you recall his lines from *Three Loves*:

My golden love is kept for two that share my fire and mat;
A little dog with simple ways, and my self-conscious cat.

Queen Victoria loved dogs and cats, her pets accompanying her on many of her travels. The cats included Persians, Angoras and Manx, as well as ordinary Black Short-hairs and Tabbies. Florence Nightingale favoured Persian cats. She always kept a large number, and named them after famous statesmen. When Miss Nightingale was permanently confined to her bedroom, her greatest relief from work was found in the companionship of cats. Often there were five or six of them in the room at once, some of them sharing her pillow.

A number of musicians have been enthusiastic over the charm of the cat. In 1757, for example, Domenico Scarlatti noticed his pet cat walking over the keys of his beloved harpsichord and was inspired to write 'The Cat's Fugue'. Later on Franz Liszt introduced it to a wider public by arranging it for the piano and playing it himself.

Another Italian composer who loved cats was Antonio Sacchini, probably best known as a writer of operas. He came to London towards the end of the eighteenth century, and lived there for ten years. Whenever he was working his two cats were to be seen sitting by his side.

But no one has ever understood the cat's nature better than the French composer, Camille Saint-Saëns. 'The cat has been most undeservedly calumniated,' he wrote; 'men will not forgive him for being proud.' He rightly claimed that certain humans thought it beneath their dignity to be forced to win the affection of the cat. He described it as 'a superior being who is conscious of his own worth and lavishes his friendship only where he knows it will be appreciated'. No animal, he declared, could be more faithful than a cat, 'once you merit his good opinion'.

Artists have always had a great affection for cats, some devoting their work almost exclusively to portraying them. One of these was Gottfried Mind, the eighteenth-century Swiss artist. He began his career by painting bears and cats, eventually specialising in cat portraiture, and became known as the 'Raphael of Cats'. It is said that he would sit for hours with a favourite cat on his knee and several kittens perched up on his shoulders. Even when he wanted to get on with his work he would never do so at the risk of disturbing his pets.

Sir Joshua Reynolds painted cats, and so did Renoir. Whistler was passionately fond of cats, and Hogarth introduced them into many of his drawings. Dame Ethel Walker kept several cats, which often travelled about with her. Wilson Steer loved not only his own cats but all the neighbouring cats of Chelsea.

Then, of course, there was Louis Wain, one-time President of the National Cat Club. Wain is remembered chiefly for his humorous drawings and brilliant caricatures of cats, but he also did some conventional cat studies. Many of his drawings were inspired by a black-and-white kitten named Peter, which had been given to him as a wedding present. He would sit for hours sketching the kitten's amusing antics and poses. Later, Louis Wain kept many other cats including Bridget, a Siamese, Leo, a Long-haired tabby, and Minna, a French cat. He was always searching for new feline models.

INDEX